ATHLONE RENAISSANCE LIBRARY

Tudor Verse Satire

ATHLONE RENAISSANCE LIBRARY

General Editors: G. BULLOUGH and C. A. MAYER

Tudor Verse Satire

selected and edited by

K. W. GRANSDEN

UNIVERSITY OF LONDON
THE ATHLONE PRESS
1970

Published by
THE ATHLONE PRESS
UNIVERSITY OF LONDON
at 2 Gower Street, London WC1

Distributed by
Tiptree Book Services Ltd
Tiptree, Essex

Australia and New Zealand
Melbourne University Press

U.S.A.
Oxford University Press Inc
New York

0 485 13601 5 *cloth*
0 485 12601 x *paperback*

Printed in Great Britain by
WESTERN PRINTING SERVICES LTD
BRISTOL

PREFACE

The present volume is intended to fill a gap in the library of the student (and general reader) of Tudor poetry, by bringing together examples of the verse-satire produced during a period of roughly a hundred years, from about 1510 to 1616 (Skelton to Jonson). Some of the poets included are, of course, available in good modern editions: readers of Spenser and Donne, however, tend to spend little time on the satires (and if a satire of Donne is anthologized it is usually the third); Marston is often anthologized in extracts; while Lodge, Gascoigne, Guilpin and Rowlands remain relatively inaccessible. A number of pieces are reprinted for the first time since the nineteenth century. So far as I know, no modern text of *Cock Lorell's Boat* or Drant's Horace has hitherto appeared.

Moreover, Tudor verse-satire is very inbred. Poets tend to imitate each other, and need to be related to their contemporaries as well as to their common models. I have tried to bring out some of these connections and also, perhaps, to place some of the more familiar pieces in a context from which they are sometimes disadvantageously divorced.

I have not attempted in the Notes to reproduce the fullness possible to the editor of a single author. But I have tried to explain difficult references and archaisms (though the *O.E.D.* remains an essential reference book) and to note sources and related passages. Wherever possible, poems are given complete; where it was a case of extracts or nothing (e.g. Spenser) these have been made as self-contained and substantial as possible. The amount of space devoted to each poet does not necessarily imply a value-judgment. Thus I do not think Lodge a better poet than Donne, but in the present context his importance seemed worth demonstrating.

The Introduction attempts a general survey of the genre. Further details of individual authors and poems are given in the Notes.

My debt to previous scholars and editors will be obvious. I should also like to thank the General Editor of this series, Professor Geoffrey Bullough, for his help in compiling and arranging this volume. I am indebted also to the following, who have helped me in matters general or particular: Professor G. K. Hunter; Sir Roger Mynors; Professor Francis Wormald; Professor G. B. A. Fletcher; Mrs Catherine Belsey; Mr Julian Roberts; and my wife, Dr Antonia Gransden.

K.W.G.

NOTE ON THE TEXT

Where the title of a poem is different from that of the volume from which it is taken, the former is normally given in the text, the latter in the Notes. In the case of nos. 6 and 7, which have no titles other than their first lines, the title of the source-volume is cited in the text. No titles have been supplied for poems not titled by their authors: in these cases, the title of the source-volume, with the number of the poem, is given at the end of the text. Bibliographical details of each poem are given in the Notes.

In modernizing the text, I have retained archaic forms (e.g. the final e) only where sense, rhyme or metre seemed to demand it. I have retained the Elizabethan spelling of 'satyre' for reasons explained in the Introduction.

CONTENTS

vii

INTRODUCTION

Satire has a long and complicated history. Satirical writing of various kinds has flourished in Europe from the time of the Greeks until the present day. In its widest sense, satire reflects the vices, absurdities and miseries of the human condition, together with the satirist's response to them. This response involves some kind of judgment, not necessarily explicit, effected by the controlled use of irony, ridicule or criticism.[1] Some of the best satirical writing is to be found in works not formally classified as satires, like the *Canterbury Tales*. Indeed, satire has often been parasitical upon other forms, so that we may speak of satirical plays or novels as well as satirical poems like those in the present volume or the satires of Dryden and Pope. In defining satire, motive, tone and attitude are better guides than structure. Orwell's *Animal Farm* may be described either as a satirical allegory or as an allegorical satire. It uses one of the oldest of literary devices, the beast-fable, also used by Spenser in *Mother Hubberd's Tale* (**9**).[2]

Satire often uses the techniques of parody and burlesque, which depend on contrasts between matter and manner. Serious matters may be treated comically, as in the plays of Aristophanes, or comic matters mock-seriously, as in Pope's *Rape of the Lock*. Ben Jonson's poem *The Famous Voyage* (**37**) satirizes both heroic epic and contemporary London by describing a voyage along the Fleet Ditch in terms of Aeneas's journey to the underworld. One of Horace's satires (II, v; cf. **4**) is a mock-epic dialogue between Ulysses and Teiresias on how to get rich, satirizing the contemporary vice of legacy-hunting by saying that the epic hero will have to endure far more 'serious' hardships in the pursuit of wealth than he ever did in his Homeric adventures. Another of Horace's satires (I, v) is a description of a journey to Brindisi, making fun of various nuisances encountered on the way. To see this poem as a satire one must clearly work with the broadest possible definition. (A modern parallel might be the letters of E. M.

[1] The most recent general survey of the whole field of satire is M. Hodgart, *Satire* (1969).
[2] These numbers refer to poems included in the present volume.

Forster, making fun both of India and of himself, in *The Hill of Devi*.) Thomas Drant, the first English translator of Horace's satires (1566), omitted the journey to Brindisi: he took the narrower (and commoner) view of satire, that it must involve the rebuking of vice, as is shown by his putting Jeremiah into the same volume as Horace, 'the one to laugh at sins, the other to weep':[3] an idea he probably got from Juvenal, who in his tenth satire contrasts Democritus, who laughed at human follies, with Heracleitus, who wept at them. Satire has always moved, sometimes uneasily, between these two polarities. To the Elizabethans, the greatest English satire was *Piers Plowman*, a work which can hardly be said (in the 'Horatian' words of Ben Jonson) 'to sport with human follies, not with crimes'.

This volume is primarily concerned with verse-satire as a literary form. But there was, of course, also a tradition of popular verse-satire in songs and ballads—burlesques, comments on contemporary affairs, 'complaints' rebuking worldliness, etc. These often anonymous works flourished alongside literary satire, in the sixteenth century as at other times.[4] Moreover, some of the liveliest Elizabethan satire is to be found in prose (notably in the works of Nashe, Greene and Lodge) and in the drama: some of Jonson's best satire is in his plays, while the reader of Marston's verse-satires should also read his play *The Malcontent* (1604), in which the hero loses his dukedom because he is too honest:

> I wanted those old instruments of state
> Dissemblance and Suspect

and adopts a 'persona' in order to 'rail' against a corrupt society in a manner closely parallel to the 'persona' of the verse-satirist.

II

The satirical poem as a literary form was, for practical purposes, invented by the Romans. In renaissance England, the verse-satires of Horace, Persius and Juvenal served as models for the 'new satire' of Wyatt and for the writers associated with the great satirical outburst of the 1590s (Donne, Hall, Marston, Guilpin).

[3] Surrey's satire against London, written in the time of Henry VIII, frequently echoes Jeremiah.
[4] See **6, 7, 11**.

We shall therefore begin with a brief survey of the relevant aspects of Latin verse-satire.

The Latin word 'satura'[5] (I shall discuss the etymology of the Elizabethan word 'satyr' later) seems originally to have meant a collection of miscellaneous poems, and later to have been used to denote a single poem of the kind we now think of as satirical, i.e. containing moral censure. But the idea of 'a satire' as a poem into which you could put anything you liked never wholly disappears.

Pre-Horatian satire need not detain us: Lucilius is important for our purposes chiefly because of what Horace says about him as his authority in the genre. Horace (Quintus Horatius Flaccus, 65 B.C.–8 B.C.) wrote two 'books' or collections of satires, containing 18 poems, the shortest of 35 lines, the longest over 300. The range is wide: character-sketches of snobs, bores, gluttons, adulterers; vivid scenes from contemporary city life; philosophical reflections on life in the country; literary discussions on the history, nature and aims of satire; and passages of autobiography, the intimate tone of which, unique in ancient literature, hardly appears in the work of his imitators (with the possible exceptions of Wyatt and Jonson). These diverse elements, often found together in the same poem, are chiefly united by an urbane and ironic wit and by the personality of the author; but the poems authoritatively establish the fact that a verse-satire could properly have an episodic and digressive structure.

Horace is important for his obsession with style, his attempts to determine the proper tone, idiom and attitudes of the genre. In *Satires*, I, x, he describes the 'mixed style' in which satire should operate: he says it should be conversational, sometimes sad, sometimes funny, sometimes poetical, sometimes rhetorical, sometimes urbane: aiming at ridicule rather than bitterness. He often uses the form of a dialogue, in which one character is a 'persona' of the poet himself; the other may be a critic, or the 'type' who is being satirized, as in the famous encounter with a bore (I, ix) which provided the model for numerous dramatized encounters with various 'types' in the verse (and prose) satire of the 1590s.[6]

[5] The spelling 'satira' is post-classical. For the origins and early meanings of the term see C. A. van Rooy, *Studies in Classical Satire and Related Literary Theory*, chs. i–iii.

[6] But English imitators (e.g. Donne, **16**) generally took only the situation from Horace, replacing his tone of amused self-mockery by one of disgust and scorn for those they meet, in the manner of Juvenal.

Horace uses the word 'satura' to describe his satirical poems (e.g. in the first line of *Satires*, II, i, see **5, 35**); but his two books bear as their title the word 'sermones', conversations. This places them in the tradition of the 'diatribes' (moralizing criticisms) of the Greek cynic philosophers.[7] Horace uses the word 'sermo' to refer not only to his books of satires but also to the two books of 'epistles' which followed them. The epistles are similar in tone, style and content to the satires proper, of which, indeed, they are (to quote Fraenkel) 'an organic continuum'. They are on the whole more reflective in tone, more polished in style and more mature in outlook than the earlier satires, but no hard and fast distinctions can be drawn. Thus *Satires*, I, vi, is virtually an epistle to Maecenas, in which the poet gives an account of his own life. Nearly all Horace's best satires are personal and reflective rather than aggressive: the poet looks inwards towards himself rather than outwards towards society. Donne's verse-letter to Wotton and Jonson's to Wroth (**17, 39**) are in the form and manner of Horatian epistles.[8] Thomas Lodge included poems labelled satires interspersed with others labelled epistles in his volume *A Fig for Momus* (1595).

Mention should also be made of Horace's *Epodes*, which, though not formally or metrically declared satires, are nevertheless frequently satirical in tone and subject, and show the range and variety of his Greek models. The second epode in particular, in praise of country life, was much imitated, but usually without the satirical ending, in which Horace deliberately undercuts the poem by revealing the speaker to be a city financier.

Horace's frequent praise of country life and his advocacy of 'withdrawal' from the corruptions and distractions of the city and court (in which he agrees with his contemporary Virgil) had a considerable influence on the renaissance: I shall say more about this when I discuss the connection between satire and pastoral. Also important to us are Horace's remarks about his predecessor Lucilius, whose reputation lay in his outspokenness: he established the *rights* of the satirist. Horace said that Lucilius attacked the town 'multa cum libertate', and also said that he was the first satirist who dared 'to strip off a man's natty (*nitidus*) exterior and

[7] For further information on Horace's Greek models see E. Fraenkel's *Horace*, J. W. Duff's *Roman Satire* and C. A. van Rooy, op. cit.

[8] But cf. also Martial, below, p. 9.

4

reveal the baseness within'. Horace claimed to follow Lucilius, and Drant said of Horace that 'with sharp satire and cutting quips' he 'could well display and dis-ease a gloser'.

This claim for the satirist's role corresponded conveniently to the Elizabethan obsession with 'dissembling', which belongs as much to Christian morality as to Stoic: cf. Christ's attack on hypocrites in Matthew 23: 'for ye are like unto whited sepulchres which indeed appear beautiful outward, but are within full of dead men's bones and of all uncleanness.' Nearly all the Elizabethan satirists make the same 'Lucilian' claim for their satires. William Rankins said his aim was 'deceptions to unbind'; Guilpin said his satires unmasked 'motley-faced dissimulation' and refers to his age as one in which men are 'blind-besotted with hypocrisy' and

> every Player-vice comes on the stage
> Masked in a virtuous role.

Asper, the 'plain-dealer' of Jonson's *Every Man Out Of His Humour*, says

> I'll strip the ragged follies of the time
> Naked, as at their birth.

And Marston's 'malcontent' says

> Well, this disguise doth yet afford me that
> Which kings do seldom hear or great men use—
> Free speech.

Horace was the first satirist to maintain that satire only hurt the guilty. These, he said, would, by the time he had done with them, be the talk of the town: 'insignis tota cantabitur urbe' (*Satires*, ii, i, 46). His claim that satire does not harm the innocent is often repeated by English satirists, from Skelton in *Colin Clout*— 'I rebuke no man that virtuous is'—to Hall in the postscript to *Virgidemiae*—'Art thou guilty? Complain not, thou art not wronged. Art thou guiltless? Complain not, thou art not touched.'

In referring to 'the town' Horace also established the essentially metropolitan nature of satire. The capital is the seat of the mighty and of the court; it contains more rogues and criminals than any other place; it is also the centre of wit and fashion, and at the beginning of the seventeenth century satire in England

5

was itself extremely fashionable. The epilogue to the play *Henry VIII* (1613) refers to those who come

> to hear the city
> Abused extremely, and to cry 'That's witty!'

Persius, Horace's successor and admirer, is also mainly a reflective and autobiographical satirist. He died, aged under thirty, in A.D. 62, leaving only six satires.[9] He saw his poetry chiefly as a means of withdrawal from the world into himself: one of his most famous phrases is 'tecum habita', live within yourself: advice echoed by Donne in his verse-letter to Sir Henry Wotton (**17**). But he is also important for emphasizing the 'biting truth' ('mordaci vero') of his poetry, thus contributing to the rather wearisome insistence of the English *fin-de-siècle* satirists on the gnawing, nagging nature of satire. Hall actually divided his satires into two groups, 'toothless' and 'biting'.

Persius's satires are more difficult, allusive and conversational even than Horace's, especially the first, though it is possible that this 'programme' satire is a deliberate bid for attention: it opens in the manner of a Horatian dialogue (cf. **5, 35**), but Persius breaks up the lines more than Horace did, and handles the hexameter more violently. He has five elisions in his first three lines:

> O curas hominum! o quantum est in rebus inane!
> 'quis leget haec?' min tu istud ais? nemo hercule. 'Nemo?'
> vel duo vel nemo. 'turpe et miserabile.' quare?

'O troubled life of men, o the emptiness of things': so the poet begins, in a parody of the typical satirist's complaint. He is at once interrupted. 'Who's going to read that kind of stuff?' 'You're asking me? No one, of course.' 'No one?' 'Well, maybe one or two people, but probably no one.' 'How rotten for you!' 'Why?' Persius here develops a technique of Horace: he goes ironically on the defensive, prepared in advance for the unpopularity of his work. Horace had affected to be 'content with a few readers' as part of his self-deprecating satirical 'persona'.[10]

Persius helped to give satire its 'private' tone and its reputation for allusiveness and obscurity. His satires were not translated

[9] A number followed, whether by accident or design, by several English *fin-de-siècle* satirists: see notes on **27, 28, 29**.

[10] For a discussion of the 'persona' of the satirist, see below, pp. 22–5.

6

complete into English until 1616, by Barten Holyday, who called his version 'a new thing, Persius understood' (Weever had translated the first satire in 1600).

Juvenal, who wrote at the beginning of the second century A.D., is the supreme exponent of 'aggressive' satire. Whereas Horace had said that he wrote because writing came naturally to him, Juvenal said that he wrote out of 'indignation', because the age required satire: the difficulty, he said, was to *avoid* writing it. This distinction is characteristic of the two poets: whereas Horace sees his poetry primarily as the expression of his own personality, Juvenal is more concerned with his subject-matter. Whereas Horace defined satire in terms of its mixed style, Juvenal defines it in terms of its mixed material: 'whatever men do, their prayers, fears, anger, pleasure, joys, distractions—of all these my book is a medley'.

Much of Juvenal's invective is directed either against the dead or at such safe stock targets as women or homosexuals. He specifically says that he will not make personal attacks on the living: he had lived through the repressive régime of the emperor Domitian and does not try to claim the 'libertas' permitted to the satirist in earlier and more liberal societies. But this does not matter, for his real subject is the total corruption and degeneration of human society. He does not need to name individuals, for we are all to blame for the human condition. In his all-embracing rhetorical questions he says, in effect, that vice is the rule not the exception:

> quis enim non vicus abundat
> tristibus obscenis?

> et quando uberior vitiorum copia?

> quis enim virtutem amplectitur ipsam
> praemia si tollas?

'What street does not overflow with sad obscenities?'

'Was there ever a more plentiful supply of vice than now?'

'Who would be virtuous unless he were paid for it?'

Juvenal's satires are not wholly negative. The famous closing lines of no. x, on what the wise man ought to desire, may be compared with some of Horace's passages against 'mempsimoiria' (discontent with one's lot); but the tone is darker; Juvenal cannot resist an ironic sneer at the superstition which masquerades as religion, yet he also conveys a sense of divine providence working for man despite all man's wickedness and folly, which is almost Christian.[11] Juvenal also had a strong sense of history, drawing on the past for moral 'exempla': his passages on the 'fall of princes' may be paralleled in medieval moral writing down to the *Mirror for Magistrates*. Above all, Juvenal had the power, possessed by few of his imitators, to strike off a memorably epigrammatic line (how many lines of Marston's satires are memorable?).

Juvenal's 'savage indignation' became the accepted pose of the English *fin-de-siècle* satirists. He combines the role of preacher, thundering denunciations against mankind in a manner at times almost medieval, with the role of sensational journalist. The opening of Guilpin's first satire:

> Shall I still mych in silence and give aim
> To other wits which make court to bright fame?

imitates the dramatic, arresting, impatient opening of Juvenal's first satire: 'Have I always got to be a listener to other poets?' Compare, too, Marston's cry of 'I cannot hold' at the beginning of his *Scourge of Villainy*, II. Perhaps the most imitated of Juvenal's satires are his third, against Rome, with its attacks on foreigners, and his sixth, on women, of which a typical echo is to be found in the following lines of Marston:

> O take compassion
> Even on your souls, make not religion
> A bawd to lewdness. Civil Socrates,
> Clip not the youth of Alcibiades
> With unchaste arms. Disguised Messaline,
> I'll tear thy mask, and bare thee to the eyes
> Of hissing boys, if to the theatre
> I find thee come once more for lecherers
> To satiate—nay, to tire thee with the use
> Of weakening lust.[12]

[11] The best-known imitation is Samuel Johnson's, but Ben Jonson's (**39**) is in some respects closer to the original.

[12] *Scourge of Villainy*, IX, 117–26. But in the phrase 'I'll tear thy mask' Marston betrays a self-consciousness about the satirist's role which is not in Juvenal (see below, pp. 22–5).

Juvenal is the most important single influence on English verse satire in the 1590s. His declamatory rhetoric, his dramatic realism, suited the malcontentism of the times. His authority and techniques provided a kind of 'cover' under which, it may be said, his English imitators (Donne, Marston, Guilpin, etc.) were able to adapt into formal verse satire the picaresque character-sketches which their contemporaries Lodge, Greene and Nashe were producing in prose-satires which derive from medieval homiletic satire and are wholly unclassical in form and manner.[13]

Juvenal describes his characters as individuals, generalizing them into types by saying that they are characteristic of a decadent society. This technique differs from the medieval one of basing a 'type' on the vice he represents, though this too has classical authority in the *Characters* of Theophrastus, a Greek prose writer of the third century B.C.: a collection of portraits of such types as the dissembler, the flatterer, the newsmonger, etc., but presented in a concrete and amusing style, closer to Nashe than to the abstract personifications of medieval allegory. Theophrastus's book appeared in a Latin version by Casaubon in 1592, and may have had some influence on the satire of the next decade, e.g. in the 'characters' of Rowlands's satires (**29–31**) though their chief source is to be found in the prose-satirists.[14] But it can be said that the two forms have natural affinities. Satire has many frontiers, of which 'character' is one; and since Elizabethan satirists were drawing on various sources, both classical and native, it is always risky to emphasize one element at the expense of others. Satire usually involves *some* element of generalization: the satirized 'type' is a vice personified and caricatured. When the transition from types to individuals is complete, we have moved from satire to fiction, in which the word 'character' has a different meaning. The works of Nashe lie somewhere on the frontier between satire and fiction: as, in our own time, can be said of the picaresque 'underworld' writings of George Orwell. The people who visit the bookshop in the first chapter of *Keep the Aspidistra Flying* are individuals satirized into types: the kind of man who likes ballet, the kind of woman who admires Hugh Walpole, etc.

One other Roman poet must be mentioned: Martial, the greatest of all exponents of the epigram, of which he wrote many

[13] For the influence of the prose-writers on verse-satire, see the Notes.
[14] See B. Boyce, *The Theophrastan Character in England to 1642*, ch. iii.

hundreds, most of them of extreme brevity (and, often, obscenity): they are related to the squib and lampoon and as such lie outside the scope of this volume. But Martial included among his epigrams a number of longer pieces, about as long as a short satire or epistle of Horace and resembling these in tone and manner, being descriptions of life in the country (contrasted with the noise and squalor of Rome). Ben Jonson's epigram 'Inviting a Friend to Supper' (**36**) is of this kind. Indeed, in Jonson's hands the epigram (to quote Herford and Simpson) 'strove, as it were, towards the miscellaneous discursiveness, the easy limits, of the epistle'. Elizabethan poets sometimes included epigrams and satires together in the same volume.

Martial was also the first poet to include an 'apology' in prose in a collection of verse of a satirical nature (in which he was followed by Hall and Marston). He prefaces his second book of epigrams with a 'letter' to Decianus in which he says that his poems need no justification and no advertisement other than their own 'ill speaking' ('mala lingua').

III

Elizabethan literature is the product of a fruitful interaction: between a renewed study of the classics (both direct, and through Italian humanism) and the continuity of the medieval tradition. Satire inspired by Christian ideals flourished in England during the middle ages and continued to influence sixteenth-century writers, including some who claimed to be following Latin models. Thus, Gascoigne invokes the authority of Lucilius in a satire (**8**) which is wholly unclassical. Medieval satire includes a large body of writing known as 'complaint': this is often allegorical, and written in a style which is abstract and general rather than concrete and particular. The term is occasionally used in our period, e.g. by Lodge, but Gascoigne prefers the word satire, by encroachment, as it were, from the classical tradition. I shall refer to this kind of satire as 'homiletic' satire, to emphasize its affinities with the sermon and the homily.[15]

[15] For the connection between medieval satire and preaching, see G. R. Owst, *Literature and Pulpit in Medieval England*, esp. chs. v, vii, viii, ix; and for the renaissance transition from complaint to satire see J. Peter, *Complaint and Satire in Early English Literature*, chs. 1–4.

Medieval satirists did not try to imitate the style or structure of classical verse-satire. But ever since that earlier humanistic renaissance, in the twelfth century, they were familiar with its content, often quoting well-known lines[16] (sometimes taken from anthologies or digests) and adapting them to their own purposes. Skelton, the first great English sixteenth-century satirist (of whom it could be said that he was born in the middle ages and died in the renaissance) pays lip-service to the four Romans in his satire 'Against Garnish', a poem which is neither homiletic nor classical:

> Thou deemest my railing overthwart;
> I rail to thee but as thou art.
> If thou wert acquainted with all
> The famous poets satirical,
> As Persius and Juvenal,
> Horace and noble Martial . . .

The poem in which these lines occur is in the medieval tradition of the 'flyting': scurrilous 'slanging-matches', addressed to named individuals, as practised by Lindsay and Dunbar. Something like it does occur in classical writing, e.g. in the scurrilous iambics of the early Greek poet Archilochus and, indeed, in Lucilius, but it is quite unlike the sophisticated techniques of formal Latin verse-satire.[17]

In his earlier work (e.g. *The Bouge of Court*) Skelton uses such medieval conventions as allegory, personified abstraction, rhyme royal and the dream or 'vision'. But in his mature satires (e.g. *Colin Clout*, **2**), while retaining the religious seriousness of the homiletic tradition, he becomes direct, concrete and polemical: his famous short line, with three stresses, interspersed with scraps of Latin, verges at times on doggerel and represents the flowering of a popular tradition.[18] In his satire against Wolsey *Why Come Ye Not to Court?* Skelton again invokes classical authority and licence.

[16] See for example a passage in the description of London in William Fitz-Stephen's *Life of Becket* (Latin, 12th cent.) which refers to satirical 'debates' between City scholars and contains quotations from the satires of Horace and Persius. For Juvenal's popularity in the middle ages, see G. Highet, *Juvenal the Satirist*, pp. 197–205.

[17] The 'pasquinades' of Italian *cinquecento* satire are also relevant here: see A. Kernan, *The Cankered Muse*, pp. 51–3, and J. Peter, op. cit., pp. 119–21.

[18] The fourteenth-century chronicle of Langtoft preserves some popular satirical songs about Edward I's wars with the Scots, which are in a similar metre.

He quotes Juvenal's famous remark, 'it is difficult to avoid writing satire', and says 'Blame Juvenal and blame not me'. But this is a mere gesture towards the classics in a poem which, while as full of indignation and aggression as Juvenal's work, is quite different in tone and structure. In a genre as complex and varied as satire, there are bound to be confusing cross-currents: the attitudes and concerns of writers operating in quite different traditions will sometimes coincide.

The chief feature of homiletic satire is its lengthy attacks on the courtly and ecclesiastical ruling-classes, in which the satirist identifies himself with the poor, the simple and the oppressed. One never feels with Skelton, as one does with Horace, that he is detached from the evils of this world, nor does one feel, as one does with Juvenal, that he is making literary capital out of them. We feel a sense of human sympathy, of concern for a social structure divided into two classes, the oppressors and the oppressed. This is the tradition of *Piers Plowman*, which the Elizabethans saw as the work of a 'malcontent', not of a religious visionary:

> Most needy are our neighbours, an we take good heed,
> As prisoners in pits, and poor folk in cots,
> Charged with children and chief-lord's rent:
> What they with spinning may spare, spend it in house-hire.
>
> (Passus X, 71–4).

Cf. Skelton's *Colin Clout*:

> What care they though Gill sweat,
> Or Jack of the Noke?
> The poor people they yoke
> With summons and citations . . .
> The bishop on his carpet
> At home full soft doth sit.

Satire against the 'estates' or classes of the community, including the religious orders, was first written in Latin in the twelfth century. In prose, the *De Nugis Curialium* of Walter Map[19] is primarily a work of court-gossip, but it also contains satirical anecdotes against certain religious orders, and its author's complaint that the frivolities and backbiting of the court make serious writing

[19] 'On the triviality of court.' The author, a clerk in the royal household of Henry II, died in 1210. The satirical poems once attributed to him are not now thought to be his.

impossible shows an acquaintance with classical satire.[20] In verse, the satires and burlesques of the so-called 'Goliards'[21] are 'anti-establishment', like modern student satire. Their style is quite unlike that of classical verse, resembling in metre and syntax the vernacular to which it would later yield. In our period, *Cock Lorell's Boat* (1) is a burlesque of this kind, in the tradition of 'rogue-literature' which we find in the ballad 'London Lickpenny' (no. 50 in R. H. Robbins, *Historical Poems of the XIVth and XVth Centuries*) and which has its last flowering in the works of Nashe, Greene, Lodge and Jonson.

After the Reformation, the church ceases to be a principal target for satire, but secular vices and follies, especially courtiers, continued to be attacked both in the homiletic manner and the picaresque (largely native, but also taking much from the classics, especially Juvenal). Thus the tone of renaissance satire varies from the bitter gibe to the earnest lamentation, from scathing realism to generalizations on the miseries of the human condition. Just before our period, the early Tudor satirist Alexander Barclay translated the German satire *Narrenschiff* into English rhyme royal under the title of *The Ship of Fools* (1508). This might be described as the last long medieval general satire, using abstract personifications and attacking the estates and the class-structure within an unrealistic framework: following a tradition which, reaching greatness in the fourteenth century with Langland, had begun to decline in the fifteenth with Lydgate.[22] Barclay's satirical *Eclogues* are in part an adaptation of a fifteenth-century anti-court satire, the *Miseriae Curialium* ('Miseries of courtiers'), of Aeneas Silvius.[23] Humanistic attacks on the court and courtiers remain a central feature of homiletic satire in the work of Gascoigne, Spenser and Lodge.

Homiletic satire is much affected by Christian *contemptus mundi* (contempt of the world). One way to defeat the princes of this world is to reflect that they will pass away. Renaissance humanists, however, sometimes sought alternatives to the corrupt life they

[20] Cf. Juvenal, *Satires*, iii and Horace, *Epistles*, ii, ii.

[21] See F. J. E. Raby, *A History of Secular Latin Poetry in the Middle Ages* (1957), ii, 89–102, 215–27.

[22] For a general survey of native satire before Barclay, see S. M. Tucker, *Verse Satire in England Before the Renaissance*, chs. i–iv.

[23] Enea Silvio de' Piccolomini, Pope Pius II, an important neo-Latin humanist author in prose and verse.

saw in the court and city. For Horace, the best alternative to
Rome was the country: which involved him in an ambivalence
towards his patron Maecenas even more tricky than that of
Spenser when he satirized the courtiers of Gloriana. One could
withdraw from the courtly world into scholarship, as Donne says
in the opening of his first satire, which carries a strong note of
contemptus mundi:

> Away, thou fondling motley humorist,
> Leave me, and in this standing wooden chest,
> Consorted with these few books, let me lie
> In prison, and here be coffined when I die.

But there is also an echo of Martial in those lines: an allusion to
the classical tradition of withdrawal, usually into the country,
taken over by Wyatt and Jonson. Jonson's poem *To Penshurst* (**38**)
uses a country estate as the image of a perfectly-adjusted society,
not 'built to envious show' like the court: a society in which is
reproduced the 'lost content' of the earthly paradise of Christian
writers or the golden age depicted by Virgil in his second *Georgic*.

The use of classical models by Christian writers inevitably in-
volved them in confusions which could not always be reconciled.
The replacement of pagan philosophy by the Christian faith
could make even the best classical models seem morally deficient.
Donne makes this point at the beginning of his third satire, using
an *a fortiori* argument to justify the use of pagan models for Chris-
tian satire:

> I must not laugh nor weep sins and be wise:[24]
> Can railing, then, cure these worn maladies?
> Is not our mistress, fair Religion,
> As worthy of all our souls' devotion
> As virtue was to the first blinded age?

During the Renaissance, humanistic attitudes appear not only
in reflective satire based on classical models but also in religious
satire of the homiletic kind. But on the whole, homiletic satirists
still identify themselves with those who have suffered from the
evils they attack, while the reflective satirist who models himself
on Horace usually appears as a self-concerned and private man,
seeking immunity, independence and self-sufficiency through a

[24] An allusion to Juvenal, perhaps via Drant's Horace (see above, p. 2).

14

Christian version of Horatian withdrawal and 'libertas'. This morality passed into Renaissance humanism not only through Horace but also through philosophical prose-writers like Cicero and Seneca: the latter's moral essays and epistles deal with the same topics as reflective satire: how to endure the 'tela fortunae' (the slings and arrows of outrageous fortune) and live according to Nature; they offer a kind of enlightened self-interest wholly foreign to the 'concern' of Skelton. The earliest reflective satire in the Horatian manner was written in Italy in the 1520s by Ariosto and Alamanni, and imitated in English in the following decade by Wyatt (see **3, 4**). The following representative passage is from Ariosto's first satire (in the first English translation, by Toft, 1608); the lines describing the poet's disappointments at court are echoed by Spenser in a satire (**9**) which is generally homiletic and un-Horatian:

> I'll only study how to gain mine ease,
> Rather than cares shall compass me about,
> And from my mind thrust contemplation out;
> Which though my body it enrich not right,
> Yet to my mind it adds such rare delight
> That it deserveth in immortal stories
> To be enrolled with all admired glories.
> And hence it comes my poverty I bear
> As it on earth my best of best things were.
> This makes that brothel wealth I do not love,
> Or that great name or titles do me move,
> Or any state allurements so adore
> That I will sell my liberty therefore.
> This makes me never to desire or crave
> What I not hope for nor am like to have. . . .
>   And sure, I think my sin is less each way,
> In this (for I respect not what men say)
> That when in court I am enforc'd to bribe
> And every scornful proud delay abide
> Ere our most lawful suits unto the Prince
> We can prefer, and be despatch'd from thence,
> Or slander honest titles or subvert
> Right without reason, conscience or desert. . . .
>   Beside, it makes me with a pure devotion
> Thank my good God for my low safe promotion;
> And that where'er I come I this have prov'd:
> I live among the best and am belov'd.

Similar passages may be found in Wyatt, whose three satires, while still influenced by Chaucerian diction, nevertheless offer a new *idea*, based on classical models, of what a verse-satire ought to be like in spirit and structure. He successfully sustains (as does Jonson later) the Horatian convention of a man talking in private to a friend, rather than shouting indignantly in public.

Wyatt's satires founded no new tradition. Meanwhile, homiletic satire continued both in prose and in the rather naïve 'drab' poetry of the earlier Elizabethans. (Skelton, alas, had no successors either: his tone was too personal, and his concerns too immediate to his own age.) Stephen Taylor's long poem *A Whip for Worldlings* (1583) is full of *contemptus mundi* and religious consolation:

> Thou art not poor: but yet suppose it so,
> In God's love richer much than many more.
> Come, art thou crooked or deformed? What then?
> Thou mayst be right in heart towards God and men . . .
> Say thou wert maimed, decrepit, ulcerous, blind:
> Thy soul is sound, sees more than most, we find.

The early complaints of Lodge are typically homiletic in tone, resembling the elegy or meditation. Sidney, discussing satire, pastoral and elegy together in his *Defence of Poesy* (1595) distinguishes the elegiac mode as that which 'would move pity rather than blame' by bewailing 'the weakness of mankind and the wretchedness of the world'. Gascoigne's *Steel Glass* (1576) (8) anticipates Spenser rather than Donne: it is a general satire against the estates; its length alone (over 1000 lines)[25] places it in the tradition of Barclay. Its central image, of the glass ('speculum') in which men may see themselves as they really are, is a commonplace of medieval writers down to Barclay and the *Mirror for Magistrates*. In prose, Gascoigne's homiletic *Drum of Doomsday* is sufficiently described by quoting the title of its medieval source: 'de contemptu mundi sive de miseria humanae conditionis' ('on contempt of the world or concerning the misery of the human condition').

The Steel Glass also makes use of a popular classical myth, the story of Philomela, from Ovid's *Metamorphoses* (also used by T. S. Eliot in *The Waste Land*). Tereus raped Philomela, then cut out her tongue so that she could not betray him; she was changed

[25] The longest classical verse-satire, Juvenal's sixth (661 lines), is nearly twice as long as any other Latin verse-satire.

into a nightingale, and her song of lamentation became a warning or example. The curious allegorical use of this myth by Gascoigne shows the connection between satire and 'exemplary' literature. Moreover, Gascoigne published with *The Steel Glass* an elegy using the same myth, *The Complaint of Philomene*, which contains moralizing rebukes against lechery:

> O whoredom, whoredom, hope for no good hap:
> The best is bad that lights on lechery;
> And (all well weighed) he sits in Fortune's lap
> Which feels no sharper scourge than beggary.
> You princes' peers, you comely courting knights,
> Which use all arts to mar the maidens' minds,
> Which win all dames with bait of fond delights,
> Which beauty force to loose what beauty binds:
> Think on the scourge that Nemesis doth bear:
> Remember this, that God (although he wink)
> Doth see all sins that ever secret were.

The homiletic tone is unmistakable. It occurs throughout the Elizabethan age, not only in literary compositions but also in numerous popular ballads which catalogue the corruptions of London, the modern Babylon, and put forth a call to reform and repentance.

IV

Something has already been said about the place of country life in the value-structure of classical satire. Renaissance poets found in the pastoral genre a convenient instrument of satire. Both genres were classified as low or humble. Both attacked the evils of court and city. The Roman critic Quintilian said of pastoral that it hated not only the forum but also the city ('non forum modo sed etiam urbem reformidat'),[26] and this could as well describe many of Horace's reflective satires, e.g. II, vi, a much imitated piece in praise of country life. In that poem Horace says 'When I have quit the city and climbed to my rural fastness, what better theme could my satires and my pedestrian muse cast lustre on?' Here, while proclaiming its humility, satire ironically corrects worldly values and makes a large moral and literary claim.

Horace's great contemporary Virgil has a famous passage in

[26] *De Institutione Oratoria*, x.

the second book of his *Georgics* satirically describing the Roman forum, 'with its wave of courtiers vomited forth from the houses of the rich', and contrasting metropolitan luxury and decadence with the peace, simplicity and morality of the country. Virgil also wrote ten short 'eclogues' or pastorals, in which the poet and his friends appear disguised as 'shepherds' celebrating the spiritual rewards of withdrawal from the world. These poems were much imitated in the Renaissance, e.g. by Spenser in *Colin Clout's Come Home Again* (**10**): but Spenser uses the convention of the eclogue to satirize the courtly world from which he has 'withdrawn'. Spenser also wrote a set of more formal eclogues, *The Shepherd's Calendar*, but even these are divided into three kinds: plaintive, recreative and moral ('which for the most part be mixed with some satirical bitterness').

Sidney in his *Defence of Poesy* voices the typical Renaissance view of the dual role of pastoral when he says that it can sometimes 'show the misery of people under hard lords' but can also express content and thankfulness by showing (as does Virgil in his first eclogue) 'what blessedness is derived to them that lie lowest from the goodness of them that sit highest'. But the kind of pastoral which concerns us here is the former, in which the poet comes before us in the 'persona' of a simple rustic criticizing the great, just as Piers Plowman or Colin Clout had done. The most important Renaissance 'eclogues' are those of Mantuan.[27] They are much longer than Virgil's, and are essentially satires disguised as pastorals. Alexander Barclay's *Eclogues* are partly modelled on Mantuan's and partly on the anti-court satire of Aeneas Silvius.[28] They are full of the commonplaces of homiletic satire:

> Of great estates there is a blinded sort,
> Which cause their sons unto the court resort,
> That they may in court themselves daily frequent,
> In learning, virtue and manners excellent:
> But better might they say, to learn all malice,
> All cursed manners and every branch of vice,
> As pride, disdain, envy and ribaldry.
> So be good manners infect with villainy,
> For surely in courts men be most vicious.

[27] Baptista Spagnoli (1447–1506), known (after his birthplace and that of his 'master' Virgil) as Mantuan, was one of the most prolific neo-Latin poets of the Italian humanist period.   [28] See above, p. 13.

Barclay presents his 'shepherds' as

> In homely language not passing their degree
> Sometimes disputing of courtly misery,

in the manner later adopted by Spenser.

The connection between pastoral and satire helps to explain the confusion among Elizabethan writers about the word 'satire'. They usually spelt it 'satyre', and connected it by a false etymology with the Greek 'satyros', a 'satyr'.[29] These grotesque creatures, half man, half beast, originated as the chorus of the ancient Greek burlesque drama. Horace describes them in his *Ars Poetica*, the most influential work of classical literary theory at this time. He identifies them with the native Roman 'fauni' or 'silvani', the gods of the woods. They were imagined as being brought on to the stage from the woods; they were 'exlex', exempt from the laws of urban civilization; they were licensed to speak in an outrageous manner.

Puttenham's account of satire in his *Art of English Poesy* (1589) is based on Horace. He sees the aim of both 'satyrs' and 'satyre' as identical: to rebuke vice; and refers (book I, ch. xiv) to 'recitals of rebuke uttered by the rural gods out of bushes and briars'. 'Satyres' soon passed into the general *décor* of renaissance pastoral; they came to represent disapproval of courtly values, and are often depicted as gloomy and unkempt, symbols of disenchantment with society. When Spenser's Timias, in *The Faerie Queene*, IV, vii, is disappointed in love, he retires into the woods and virtually becomes a 'satyre'. In his poem *The Discontented Satyre* (**13**) Lodge creates a personification of critical discontent; and William Rankins, in the eight-line 'induction' to his *Seven Satyres* (1599), shows how 'satyres' could personify satirical poems and embody a critical attitude to society in pastoral terms:

> Of love, of courtships, and of fancy's force,
> Some gilded Braggadocchio may discourse:
> My shaggy satyres do forsake the woods,
> Their beds of moss, their unfrequented floods,
> Their marble cells, their quiet forest life,
> To view the manner of this human strife.
> Whose skin is touched, and will in gall revert,
> My satyres vow to gall them at the heart.

[29] This confusion was cleared up by Isaac Casaubon in his important, and carefully titled, essay *De Satyrica Graecorum Poesi et Romanorum Satira* (1605).

Rankins's reference to Braggadocchio, the character in *The Faerie Queene* (II, iii) who uses false rhetoric to argue that the court is a better place than the country, shows that he connected 'satyres' with Spenserian pastoral, in which phrases like 'beds of moss', deriving from Virgilian pastoral (in which they indicate a 'good' simplicity) are common. Rankins also refers to Fauns, whom he calls 'nimble companions of our silvan court'. Thus Horace's burlesque satyrs, which he had regarded merely as a piece of literary history, assume in the Renaissance a much greater significance. But the traditional burlesque element also remained: as witness Samuel Rowlands in *The Letting of Humour's Blood in the Head-Vein* (1600), a collection of epigrams and satires: at the end of the epigrams Rowlands writes 'Enter goat-footed satyres, butt like rams'.

The unkemptness and roughness of 'satyres' also contributed to the idea prevalent among English satirists at the end of the sixteenth century that satire ought to be rough and harsh. Just as its attitudes were the reverse of courtly 'seeming', so its versification ought to be the reverse of smooth and elegant. The 'satyre' thus personified not only an attitude but also a style.[30] But another confusion now arises. A rough harsh style should be plain and outspoken, befitting an uncourtly 'satyr' who says what he means. But Elizabethan satirists found Latin satire difficult both because of its obscure allusions and because its style seemed less smooth than that of Virgil; so that 'rough' and 'harsh' came to mean 'dark' and 'difficult'. They were aided in this confusion by their belief that in Latin satire a 'rough' style was adopted in order to conceal the true meaning. William Webbe, in his *Discourse of English Poesy* (1586) says that 'Horace is a poet not of the smoothest style'; four years earlier, in the preface to his translation of the first four books of Virgil's *Aeneid*, Richard Stanyhurst unfavourably contrasts Virgil's polished style with the poetry of the three Roman satirists, of whom he says: 'their verses, camfering-wise, run harsh and rough, performing nothing in matter but biting quips, taunting darkly certain men of state, besprinkling their invectives with some moral precepts, answerable to the capacity of every weak brain.'

Finding their Latin models difficult in style and obscure in

---

[30] Puttenham says (op. cit., I, xi) that the satirist's aim was 'to tax the common abuses and vices of the people in rough and bitter speeches'.

allusion, English satirists concluded that it was the proper nature of the genre to be 'rough', 'harsh' and 'dark'. Hall and Marston actually apologize to the reader for not being as obscure as their 'antique' models. Hall, however, while agreeing about the style of classical satire, saw as virtues what Stanyhurst saw as faults: 'satyre', he says, 'is both hard of conceit and harsh of style, and therefore cannot but be unpleasing to the unskilful and over-musical ear'. In the prologue to *Virgidemiae*, iii, Hall blames the vernacular for his failure to live up to the high standard of obscurity set by his models:

> Some say my satyrs over-loosely flow,
> Nor hide their gall enough from open show:
> Not riddle-like obscuring their intent,
> But pack-staff plain, uttering what thing they meant;
> Contrary to the Roman ancients,
> Whose words were short, and darksome was their sense.
> Who reads one line of their harsh poesies,
> Thrice must he take his wind, and breathe him thrice.
> My muse would follow them that have foregone,
> But cannot with an English pinion:
> For look how far the ancient comedy
> Passed former satyrs in her liberty:
> So far must mine yield unto them of old:
> 'Tis better to be bad than to be bold.

Hall's lines are probably an imitation of the defence of satire by Horace at the beginning of *Satires*, ii, i (see **5, 35**). But whereas Horace is merely complaining, half-seriously, that whatever style the satirist adopts he will still make enemies, Hall assumes that the supposed obscurity of his Latin models was a deliberate exercise in camouflage in order to obtain greater freedom.

Marston, however, in the preface to his *Scourge of Villainy*, says that, although he wrote his first satire in the belief that his classical models were deliberately obscure, he now feels this view—held, he says, by 'too many'—to be wrong: it is merely that ancient satire is remote from us. Nevertheless, Marston's earlier satires offer several examples of confusion between matter and manner, between 'darkness' of purport and 'darkness' of style. In *Certain Satyres*, ii, he asks:

> Help to unmask the satyre's secrecy:
> Delphic Apollo, aid me to unrip

These intricate deep oracles of wit,
These dark enigmas and strange riddling sense
Which pass my dullard brain's intelligence.

It is characteristic of much English satire at this time to show
more concern with revealing the truth about the genre itself than
with revealing the truth about the evils it was supposed to be
'unmasking'.[31] This concern is partly the result of the current
interest in classical literary theory. However, many of the most
entertaining satires of the period remain largely unaffected by
these preoccupations.

V

Of all literary genres, satire has always by its nature been the most
vulnerable. As Ben Jonson says in *Epigrams*, xciv (addressed to the
Countess of Bedford with a copy of Donne's satires)

> since the most of mankind be
> Their unavoided subject

only very good people will enjoy reading them. The rest of us
may be less accommodating; and Renaissance satirists (like their
predecessors) frequently defend themselves and justify their
motives. A common line of defence was self-deprecation. The
genre was, as has been said, classified as 'humble': partly because
of its informal style and partly because the satirist frequently
came before the reader as a 'plain dealer', a homely and critical
rustic like Piers Plowman, Colin Clout, or Barclay's 'shepherds'.
In the lines from Hall quoted above, the satirist ironically apolo-
gizes for using a plain and straightforward vernacular. As it
happens, Horace had called his satires 'earthbound' and 'pedes-
trian', ironically distinguishing them from grand and inspired
poetry (like epic), but their style, though idiomatic, is neither
plain nor rude, but extremely sophisticated. Hall's claim, how-
ever, is in the native tradition of Skelton (the first English satirist
self-consciously to proclaim his plain style) and Spenser, who
called the style of *Mother Hubberd's Tale* 'base' and its matter
'mean'.

Not surprisingly, however, the satirist's self-defensiveness did
not always win for him the immunity he sought. Indeed, the

[31] Cf. the lines from Marston, *Scourge of Villainy*, ix, quoted above, p. 8.

irony with which the defence is often conducted is in itself a kind of preparation for possible reprisals. Skelton could not get *Colin Clout* printed;[32] and in 1599, at the height of the *fin-de-siècle* fashion for satire, a number of publications, including those of Marston, were called in and burnt: although the reason seems to have been primarily obscenity rather than moral outspokenness (many classical satires are obscene and some English imitators undoubtedly took advantage of what they felt to be a safely established convention).[33]

Thus the satirist adopted a 'mask': either he paraded a kind of bluff honesty, or a disarming innocence;[34] or he was a man licensed to attack society by a long-established literary tradition with classical authority behind it. He wanted to be taken seriously and yet not seriously at the same time. Horace defended his satires on aesthetic grounds, expecting people (in Auden's words) to 'pardon him for writing well'. Some satirists defended themselves by saying that their work was made necessary by the widespread corruption of society; others argued (with Lodge) that they did not 'really' attack anyone but only affected to do so 'to observe the laws of this kind of poem'. Thus in various ways the satirist might show himself not wholly at ease with his genre: a certain self-consciousness might appear, as in these lines from Jonson's 'Epistle to Lady Aubigny' (*Forest*, xiii):

> I therefore, who profess myself in love
> With every virtue, wheresoe'er it move
> And howsoever: as I am at feud
> With sin and vice, though with a throne endued,
> And in this name am given out dangerous
> By arts and practice of the vicious,
> Such as suspect themselves, and think it fit
> For their own capital crimes to indict my wit.

Once you start to pass moral judgments, you become involved: and it may not be enough to offer sophisticated literary distinctions between the 'satyre' as a 'persona' and the satirist as a man.

[32] See **2**, lines 1236 ff.

[33] For details of this censorship, see J. Peter, op. cit., pp. 147–52 and Davenport's edition of Hall, p. xxvi and Appendix III. Hall's own satires were in fact reprieved.

[34] This 'mask' occurs even in popular ballads, e.g. in the anti-Reformation satirical ballad 'Little John Nobody' (*temp.* Edward VI) in which the speaker says he is 'little John Nobody that durst not speak'.

In *Certain Satyres*, II, Marston shows that he is aware of the satirist's shaky moral ground. The fact that the world continues to be corrupt shows how little effect satire has. Marston here says that he will not claim the conventional innocence of the 'satyre':

> But since myself am not immaculate,
> But many spots my mind doth vitiate,
> I'll leave the white robe and the biting rhymes
> Unto our modern satyre's sharpest lines,
> Whose hungry fangs snarl at some secret sin.

This attitude makes its last memorable appearance in English verse-satire in Byron's lines in *English Bards and Scotch Reviewers*, where the poet says he has adopted the role of satirist by default —because no one who is both a good poet and a good man (the play on aesthetic and moral criteria is neatly adapted from Horace) has come forward. It is the end of a tradition:

> E'en I—least thinking of a thoughtless throng,
> Just skilled to know the right and choose the wrong,
> Freed at that age when reason's shield is lost
> To fight my course through passion's countless host:
> Whom every path of pleasure's flowery way
> Has lured in turn, and all have led astray—
> E'en I must raise my voice, e'en I must feel
> Such scenes, such men, destroy the public weal:
> Although some kind, censorious friend will say
> 'What, art thou better, meddling fool, than they?'
> And every brother-rake will smile to see
> That miracle, a moralist in me.

Satire also tried to justify itself by attacking other literary forms, claiming that it alone was truthful. Juvenal begins his first satire by contemptuously rejecting the epics and tragedies of his contemporaries. Hall attacks other genres in the first book of *Virgidemiae* (see **19**); Guilpin in the 'praeludium' to his *Skialetheia* rejects 'whimpering sonnets' and 'puling elegies' and even 'the stateliest and most heroic poetry' as 'lascivious'. He goes on:

> The satyre only and epigrammatist
> Keep diet from this surfeit of excess . . .
> Are antidotes to pestilential sins.

This over-compensation is perhaps the other side of the coin to the self-defensiveness mentioned above. The argument is that only satire can meet the total needs of society. Guilpin calls satire the 'Tamburlaine of vice'. We see here a glimpse of the all-conquering form which satire was to become in the following two centuries. But its immediate victories were more precarious. After the ban on satire in 1599 we find John Weever, in *The Whipping of the Satyre* (1601), attacking satirists, epigrammatists and humourists, 'those three vessels of iniquity', for the way in which they 'lay open the infirmities of their countrymen'. Weever asks indignantly

> Is it not villainy
> That one should live by reckoning up of vice,
> And be a sin-monger professedly,
> Involuming offences for a price?

Weever's poem is a typical piece of opportunism. If satire were denied all other targets, it could still attack itself, and in so doing covertly continue the 'aggressive' tradition. In another poem (32) Weever says that all the vices which the satirist used to attack are disappearing, and then proceeds to attack them again under a new 'mask'—that of the parodist. The argument about the moral justification of satire was continued by Breton and Guilpin (see Davenport's edition of the 'Whipper' poems): Guilpin's answer to Weever's 'recantation' is that 'a true satyre's guiltless of transgression' and

> may not be deposed
> So long as Truth sings his apology.

And this remained, on the whole, it as had always been, the central position of English satire. In our own century, Wyndham Lewis claimed that 'satire is nothing else but the truth, in fact that of natural science . . . for it has been bent not so much upon pleasing as upon being true'.[35]

VI

During the seventeenth century verse-satire gradually shed some of the confusions and preoccupations of the sixteenth. 'Complaint' went out of fashion; satire became wittier, smoother, more sophisticated. The decasyllabic or 'heroic' couplet—in our period

[35] See *Men Without Art* (1934). For a discussion of Lewis's view of satire, which often reaffirms that of Renaissance satirists, see R. C. Elliott, *The Power of Satire*, pp. 223–37.

merely one of several metres used for satire—began to oust all rivals. Its possibilities as an instrument for witty antithesis—in the manner later to be called Augustan—were to some extent exploited by Hall, Lodge, Rowlands and Jonson, but nowhere better than by Shakespeare in *Othello*, II, i, where Iago ('I am nothing if not critical') speaks on the 'topic' of women: the licensed 'bluff' entertainer sends 'the old fond paradoxes' trippingly off the tongue 'to make fools laugh i' the alehouse':

> She that was ever fair, and never proud,
> Had tongue at will, and yet was never loud,
> Never lack'd gold, and yet went never gay,
> Fled from her wish, and yet said 'Now I may';
> She that being angered, her revenge being nigh,
> Bade her wrong stay, and her displeasure fly;
> She that in wisdom never was so frail
> To change the cod's head for the salmon's tail;
> She that could think, and ne'er disclose her mind,
> See suitors following and not look behind;
> She was a wight, if ever such wight were—
> To suckle fools and chronicle small beer.

The wit here is largely determined by the metrical structure. We find nothing quite like it again until Pope:

> She who can love a sister's charms, or hear
> Sighs for a daughter with unwounded ear;
> She who ne'er answers till a husband cools,
> Or, if she rules him, never shows she rules;
> Charms by accepting, by submitting sways,
> Yet has her humour most when she obeys.
>
> (*Moral Essays*, II, 259–64.)

Whenever Renaissance satire makes a gesture towards Augustan wit and poise it does so by exploiting the couplet. The process of smoothing out this metre was continued by Waller, Denham and Dryden and completed by Pope (whose 'versified', i.e. modernized, version of Donne's fourth satire may instructively be compared with the original). This process involved also a smoothing-out of the whole concept of satire, a shedding of its medieval and 'metaphysical' elements (though these survive as late as Rochester, whose satires look forward to the Augustans and back to Donne). What emerged was a synthesis of Horatian poise and Juvenalian aggression. Such a synthesis lies beyond the limits of this volume.

But the following lines from Lord Mulgrave's *Essay on Poetry*
(1691) seem worth quoting, if only because to the general reader
verse-satire means Dryden and Pope—in whose work an aggres-
sion as superbly arrogant as Juvenal's or Marston's is controlled
by a literary sensibility as 'delicate' and 'nice' as Horace's. The
lines also show the persistence of the personified 'satyre' and of the
idea that satire should be rough:

> Satyr well writ has most successful prov'd,
> And cures because the remedy is lov'd.
> 'Tis hard to write on such a subject more,
> Without repeating things oft said before.
> Some vulgar errors only we remove
> That stain a beauty which so much we love.
> Of well-chose words some take not care enough,
> And think they should be as the subject rough.
> This great work must be more exactly made,
> And sharpest thoughts in smoothest words convey'd.
> Some think if sharp enough they cannot fail,
> As if their only business were to rail.
> But human frailty nicely to uphold
> Distinguishes a satyr from a scold.
> Rage you must hide and prejudice lay down:
> A satyr's smile is sharper than his frown.

The interesting point here is that a smooth style and a smooth
definition of satire go hand in hand. One may say that the rise of
the heroic couplet as the dominant metre and the rise of satire as
the dominant genre (in its widest sense, to include burlesque and
travesty and the moral 'essay' or epistle) go hand in hand. In his
poem on Milton's *Paradise Lost* Marvell praises Milton for eschew-
ing the 'tinkling' fashion of rhyme, yet he himself couches his
panegyric in couplets, admitting 'I too, transported by the mode,
offend'. The couplet was, of course, a native English metre, used
by Chaucer and later by Barclay, by Spenser in his neo-medieval
Mother Hubberd's Tale and by Stephen Taylor in *A Whip for
Worldlings*. But before 1600 many experiments were made in
English prosody, and it remains to add a note on some of the
other metres used in Renaissance satire.

Wyatt borrowed his *terza rima* from the Italians.[36] Gascoigne
used blank verse for *The Steel Glass*, an innovation to which he

---

[36] Surrey uses octosyllabic *terza rima* for his 'London' satire.

draws attention rather self-consciously in his preface ('this satire written without rhyme but, I trust, not without reason'). This metre was also borrowed from Italy, first by Surrey some thirty years before, for his translation of part of the *Aeneid*. As handled by Gascoigne, it has a heavy monotonous ring. Gascoigne was one of the chief early Elizabethan regularisers of metre. His blank verse has frequent alliteration and a strong caesura after the fourth syllable of nearly every line (a practice he himself recommends in his 'Certain Notes of Instruction on English Prosody'). The variations of stress *vis-à-vis* the metrical pattern, the living speech-rhythms and medieval pronunciations of Wyatt and Skelton, were suppressed from the time of *Tottel's Miscellany* (1557) in which Wyatt's satires were first printed, and a regular decasyllabic line of five iambics substituted. This iambic regularity was later deliberately broken up again in the couplets of Donne and Marston in a self-conscious attempt to imitate the 'irregular' hexameters of Latin satire.

In some of his other long poems, Gascoigne uses a decasyllabic line with alternate rhymes, which Spenser took over for *Colin Clout's Come Home Again*. This metre has only to be printed as quatrains to become the familiar metre of Gray's *Elegy*.

Drant translated Horace's satires into the rhymed 'fourteener' couplet, a clumsy but popular measure also used by Edward Hake in his early and tedious collection of satires *News Out of Paul's Churchyard* (1567). The fourteener was used by Chapman for his translation of Homer's *Iliad*, but he abandoned it in favour of the heroic couplet when he came to translate the *Odyssey*. Metres are subject to the law of the survival of the fittest. The fourteener was to survive chiefly as the so-called 'common metre' of English hymnody, for which purpose it was (as Gascoigne pointed out) admirably suited. Each fourteener was divided into two lines of eight and six syllables respectively and printed thus:

> While shepherds watched their flocks by night,
> All seated on the ground,
> The angel of the Lord came down
> And glory shone around.

Two other metres remain to be mentioned. The seven-line stanza known as rhyme royal (ababbcc), used by Chaucer and Lydgate, was taken over for homiletic satire by Barclay, Skelton,

Lodge, Breton, Rankins and the *Mirror for Magistrates*. It was also used for Ovidian erotic elegy, e.g. by Shakespeare in *The Rape of Lucrece*. A six-line stanza was similarly used: by Shakespeare in *Venus and Adonis*, by Lodge, Breton and Weever, and also by Marston, in his erotic satire *Pygmalion* and in some of his verse prefaces; but he used the couplet for his satires proper, following the lead given by Donne, Hall and (in *A Fig for Momus* but not in his earlier volumes) Lodge.

BIBLIOGRAPHY

Details of editions and critical studies of the individual poets represented in this anthology are given in the Notes. References in the Notes to Nashe's works are to R. B. McKerrow's edition, revised F. P. Wilson (1958). The books listed below will be found helpful by those who wish to explore further the points raised in the Introduction.

I. *Background*

Lewis, C. S., *English Literature in the Sixteenth Century* (Oxford, 1954)
Owst, G. R., *Literature and Pulpit in Medieval England* (repr. Oxford, 1961)
Smith, Gregory (ed.), *Elizabethan Critical Essays* (Oxford, 1917)

II. *Classical Satire*

Duff, J. W., *Roman Satire* (Cambridge, 1937)
Fraenkel, E., *Horace* (Oxford p.b., 1966)
Highet, G., *Juvenal the Satirist* (Oxford p.b., 1962)
Rudd, N., *The Satires of Horace* (Cambridge, 1966)
Sullivan, J. P. (ed.), *Critical Essays in Roman Literature: Satire* (London, 1963)
Van Rooy, C. A., *Studies in Classical Satire and Related Literary Theory* (Leiden, 1965)

III. *Renaissance Satire*

Alden, R. M., *The Rise of Formal Satire in England* (Philadelphia, 1899)
Boyce, B., *The Theophrastan Character in England to 1642* (Cambridge, Mass., 1947)
Judges, A. V., *The Elizabethan Underworld* (London, 1930)
Kernan, A., *The Cankered Muse* (New Haven, 1959)
Peter, J., *Complaint and Satire in Early English Literature* (Oxford, 1956)
Tucker, S. M., *Verse Satire in England Before the Renaissance* (1909; repr. New York, 1966)

IV. *Satire in General*

Elliott, R. C., *The Power of Satire* (Princeton, 1960)
Hodgart, M., *Satire* (London p.b., 1969)

Cock Lorell's Boat

Then came one with two bulldogs at his tail,   43
And that was a butcher without fail,
All begored in red blood;
In his hand he bare a flap for flies,
His hosen greasy upon his thighs
(That place for maggots was very good);
On his neck he bare a coulter log,
He had as much pity as a dog   50
And he were once wroth:
He looked peevish and also rough,
A man would take him for a shrew, I trow,
And of his company be loth.
Then came a gong-farmer
(Otherwise called a masser-scourer);
With him a channel-raker—
Their presence made Cock and his men to spew,
For as sweet was their breath as henkam or rue;
To wash them they lacked water.   60
On these Irish couple I will not tarry;
Cock did set them there as knaves should be,
Among the slovenly sort.
Then came two false tollers in next,
He set them by pickers of the best,
For there should they abide;
But before that they were plunged in the river,
To search their bodies fair and clear:
Thereof they had good sport.
A miller dusty-poll then did come,   70
A jolly fellow with a golden thumb;
On his neck a sack was;
Many said that he with reproof
Of all crafts was next a thief;
In that Cock found no lack;
He said that he tolled twice for forgetting,

31

And stole flour and put chalk therein—
Beshrew him that taught him that!
Cock bade him grind cherry-stones and peason
To make his men bread for a season   80
Because wheat was very dear.
Then came a pardoner with his book;
His quarterage of every man he took,
But Cock would their names hear.
The pardoner said, 'I will read my roll,
And ye shall hear the names poll by poll,
Thereof ye need not fear.
Here is first Cock Lorell the knight,
And Symkyn Emery, maintenance again right;
With Slingthrift, fleshmonger;   90
Also Fabian, flatterer,
And Fesly, clatterer,
With Adam Averus, flail-swinger;
And Francis Flaproach, of stews captain late,
With Giles Unyeste, mayor of Newgate,
And Lewis Unlusty the leasing-monger;
Here also Baud Baudyn, boller,
And his brother Copyn Coler,
With Matthew Marchaunt of Shooter's Hill,
Christopher Catchpoll a-Christ's corse, gatherer,   100
And Wat Welbelyne of Ludgate, jailor,
With Laurence Lorell of Clerkenwell.'

   . . . .

Cock said, 'Pardoner, now ho and cease,   145
Thou makest me weary, hold thy peace.
A thing tell thou me:
What profit is to take thy pardon?
Show us what meed is to come
To be in this fraternity?'   150
'Sir, this pardon is new-found
Beside London Bridge in a holy ground,
Late called the stews' bank.
Ye know well all, that there was
Some religious women in that place
To whom men offered many a frank;

And because they were so kind and liberal
A marvellous adventure there is befall,
If ye list to hear how.
There came such a wind from Winchester   160
That blew these women over the river,
In wherry, as I will you tell.
Some at Saint Katherine's struck aground,
And many in Holborn were found;
Some at Saint Giles, I trow,
Also in Ave Maria alley and at Westminster,
And some in Shoreditch drew thither
With great lamentation.
And because they have lost that fair place
They will build at Coleman-hedge in space   170
Another noble mansion,
Fairer 'n' ever the half-street was.
For every house new paved is with grass,
Shall be full of fair flowers,
The walls shall be of hawthorn, I wot well,
And hanged with white motley that sweet doth smell;
Green shall be the colours.
And as for this old place, these wenches holy,
They will not have it called the stews for folly,
But maketh it a strawberry bank;   180
And there is yet a chapel safe
Of which ye all the pardon have
(The saint is of Symme Trollanke).
I will rehearse here in general
The indulgences that ye have shall—
Is these that followeth, with more:
At the hour of death, when ye have need,
Ye shall be absolved of every good deed
That you have done before;
And ye shall be partaker of as many good deed   190
As is done every night abed;
And also furthermore,
At every tavern in the year
A solemn *dirige* is sung there
With a great drinking;
At all ale-houses truly

Ye shall be prayed for heartily
With a joyful weeping.'

.   .   .   .

Then Cock Lorell did his whistle blow,   347
That all his men should him know;
With that they cried and made a shout,
That the water shook all about;   350
Then men might hear the oars clash,
And on the water gave many a dash.
They spread their sails as void of sorrow,
Forth they rode Saint George to borrow.
For joy their trumpets they did blow,
And some sung heave and ho rumbelow.
They sailed from Garlic Head to Knaves' Inn,
And a peal of guns 'gan they ring;
Of Coleman-hedge a sight they had,
That made his company very glad,   360
For there they thought all to play
Between Tyburn and Chelsea.
With this man was a lusty company,
For all rascals from them they did try;
They banished prayer, peace and sadness,
And took with them mirth, sport and gladness;
They would not have virtue, ne yet devotion,
But riot and revel, with jolly rebellion.
They sung and danced full merrily,
With swearing and staring heaven-high.   370
Some said they were gentlemen of great might,
That their purses were so light;
And some went in furred gowns, and gay shoon,
That had no more faces than had the moon.
Of this day glad was many a brothel,
That might have an oar with Cock Lorell;
Thus they danced with all their might
Till that Phoebus had lost his light.
But then came Lucina with all her pale hue
To take her sport among the clouds blue;   380
And Mercury he threw down his golden beams
And Sperus her silver streams,

34

That in the world gave so great light
As all the earth had been paved with white.
Then Cock weighed anchor and hoised his sail,
And forth he rode without fail;
They sailed England thorough and thorough,
Village, town, city and borough;
They blessed their ship when they had done,
And drank about Saint Julian's turn.   390
Then every man pulled at his oar,
With that I could see them no more:
But as they rowed up the hill
The boatswain blew his whistle full shrill;
And I went homeward to mow, shame, stir.
With a company I did meet,
As eremites, monks and friars,
Chanons, charterers and innholders,
And many white nuns with white veils
That was full wanton of their tales.   400
To meet with Cock they asked how to do,
And I told them he was a-gone;
Then were they sad everyone,
And went again to their home;
But my counsel I gave them there,
To meet with Cock another year.
    No more of Cock now I write:
But merry it is when knaves done meet;
Cock had in his hand a great rout,
The third person of England.   410
Thus of Cock Lorell I make an end,
And to heaven God your souls send
That readeth this book over all;
Christ cover you with his mantle perpetual.

35

2 · JOHN SKELTON

Colin Clout

And if ye stand in doubt 47
Who brought this rhyme about,
My name is Colin Clout.
I purpose to shake out 50
All my conning bag,
Like a clerkly hag;
For though my rhyme be ragged,
Tattered and jagged,
Rudely rain-beaten,
Rusty and moth-eaten,
If ye take well therewith
It hath in it some pith.
For, as far as I can see,
It is wrong with each degree: 60
For the temporalty
Accuseth the spiritualty;
The spiritual again
Doth grudge and complain
Upon the temporal men:
Thus each of other blother
The one against the t'other:
Alas, they make me shudder!
For in hoder-moder
The Church is put in fault; 70
The prelates ben so haut,
They say, and look so high,
As though they would fly
Above the starry sky.

.   .   .

Thus I, Colin Clout, 287
As I go about,
And wandering as I walk
I hear the people talk.
Men say, for silver and gold 290
Mitres are bought and sold;
There shall no clergy appose
A mitre nor a crose,

But a full purse:
A straw for God's curse!
What are they the worse?
For a simoniac
Is but a hermoniac;
And no more ye make 300
Of simony, men say,
But a child's play.
  Over this, the foresaid lay
Report how the Pope may
An holy anchor call
Out of the stony wall,
And him a bishop make,
If he on him dare take
To keep so hard a rule,
To ride upon a mule 310
With gold all betrapped,
In purple and pall belapped;
Some hatted and some capped,
Richly and warm bewrapped,
God wot, to their great pains,
In rochets of fine Rennes,
White as morrow's milk;
Their tabards of fine silk,
Their stirrups with gold begared:
There may no cost be spared; 320
Their mules gold doth eat,
Their neighbours die for meat.
  What care they though Gill sweat,
Or Jack of the Noke?
The poor people they yoke
With summons and citations
And excommunications,
About churches and market:
The bishop on his carpet
At home full soft doth sit. 330

     .   .   .   .

Ye are so puffed with pride 595
That no man may abide
Your high and lordly looks:

Ye cast up then your books
And virtue is forgotten;
For then ye will be wroken 600
Of every light quarrel
And call a lord a javel;
A knight a knave ye make,
Ye boast, ye face, ye crake,
And upon you ye take
To rule both king and kaiser;
And if ye may have leisure
Ye will bring all to nought,
And that is all your thought:
For the lords temporal, 610
Their rule is very small,
Almost nothing at all.
Men say how ye appal
The noble blood royal
In earnest and in game;
Ye are the less to blame,
For lords of noble blood,
If they well understood
How conning might them advance,
They would pipe you another dance. 620
But noble men born
To learn they have scorn,
But hunt and blow an horn,
Leap over lakes and dykes,
Set nothing by politics;
Therefore ye keep them base,
And mock them to their face.
This is a piteous case!
To you that be on the wheel
Great lords must crouch and kneel, 630
And break their hose at the knee,
As daily men may see
And to remembrance call;
Fortune so turneth the ball
And ruleth so over all,
That honour hath a great fall.

. . . .

But now my mind ye understand,   889
For they must take in hand
To preach, and to withstand
All manner of abjections;
For bishops have protections,
They say, to do corrections,
But they have no affections
To take the said directions.
In such manner of cases,
Men say, they bear no faces
To occupy such places,
To sow the seed of graces: 900
Their hearts are so fainted
And they be so attainted
With covetous ambition,
And other superstition,
That they be deaf and dumb,
And play silence and glum,
Can say nothing but mum.
    They occupy them so
With singing *Placebo*,
They will no farther go: 910
They had liefer to please
And take their worldly ease,
Than to take on hand
Worshipfully to withstand
Such temporal war and bate
As now is made of late
Against holy Church estate,
Or to maintain good quarrels.
The laymen call them barrels
Full of gluttony   920
And of hypocrisy,
That counterfeits and paints
As they were very saints.
In matters that them like
They show them politic,
Pretending gravity
And seniority
With all solemnity

For their indemnity.
For they will have no loss
Of a penny nor of a cross
Of their predial lands,
That cometh to their hands,
And as far as they dare set
All is fish that cometh to net;
Building royally
Their mansions curiously,
With turrets and with towers,
With hallès and with bowers
Stretching to the stars
With glass windows and bars;
Hanging about the walls
Cloths of gold and palls,
Arras of rich array,
Fresh as flowers in May;
With Dame Diana naked;
How lusty Venus quaked,
And how Cupid shaked
His dart, and bent his bow
For to shoot a crow
At her tirly-tirlo;
And how Paris of Troy
Danced a *lege de moy*,
Made lusty sport and joy
With dame Helen the queen;
With such stories bydene
Their chambers well beseen,
With triumphs of Caesar
And of Pompeius' war,
Of renown and of fame
By them to get a name.
How all the world stares,
How they ride in goodly chairs,
Conveyed by elephants
With laureate garlants,
And by unicorns
With their seemly horns;
Upon these beasts riding,

930

940

950

960

Naked boys striding,
With wanton wenches winking.
Now truly, to my thinking,
That is a speculation
And a meet meditation
For prelates of estate,
Their courage to abate
From worldly wantonness,
Their chambers thus to dress
With such perfectness
And all such holiness.
Howbeit they let down fall
Their churches cathedral.
   Squire, knight and lord
Thus the Church remord;
With all the temporal people
They run against the steeple,
Thus talking and telling
How some of you are melling;
Yet soft and fair for swelling,
Beware of a queen's yelling.
It is a busy thing
For one man to rule a king
Alone, and make reckoning
To govern over all
And rule a realm royal
By one man's very wit.
Fortune may chance to flit,
And when he weeneth to sit
Yet may he miss the cushion;
For I rede a proposition:
Cum regibus amicare
Et omnibus dominari,
Et supra te pravare.
Wherefore he hath good ure
That can himself assure
How fortune will endure.
Then let reason you support,
For the commonalty report
That they have great wonder

That ye keep them so under;
Yet they marvel so much less, 1010
For ye play so at the chess,
As they suppose and guess,
That some of you but late
Hath played so checkmate
With lords of great estate,
After such a rate,
That they shall mell nor make,
Nor upon them take
For king nor kaiser's sake,
But at the pleasure of one 1020
That ruleth the roost alone.
    Helas, I say, helas!
How may this come to pass,
That a man shall hear a mass
And not so hardy on his head
To look on God in form of bread,
But that the parish clerk
Thereupon must hark
And grant him at his asking
For to see the sacring? 1030
    And how may this accord?
No man to our sovereign lord
So hardy to make suit,
Nor yet to execute
His commandment
Without the assent
Of your president,
Nor to express to his person
Without your consentation
Grant him his licence 1040
To press to his presence,
Nor to speak to him secretly,
Openly nor privily
Without his president be by
Of else his substitute
Whom he will depute?
Neither earl ne duke
Permitted? By saint Luke,

And by sweet saint Mark,
This is a wondrous work!
That the people talk this,
Somewhat there is amiss:
The devil cannot stop their mouths
But they will talk of such uncouths,
All that ever they ken
Against all spiritual men.
　　Whether it be wrong or right,
Or else for despite,
Or however it hap,
Their tongues thus do clap,
And through such detraction
They put you to your action;
And whether they say truly
As they may abide thereby,
Or else that they do lie,
Ye know better than I.
But now *debetis scire*
And groundly *audire*,
In your *convenire*,
Of this praemunire,
Or else in the mire
They say they will you cast:
Therefore stand sure and fast.
Stand sure, and take good footing,
And let be all your mooting,
Your gazing and your toting,
And your partial promoting
Of those that stand in your grace;
But old servants ye chase
And put them out of their place.
Make ye no murmuration,
Though I write after this fashion;
Though I, Colin Clout,
Among the whole rout
Of you that clerkès be
Take now upon me
Thus copiously to write,
I do it for no despite.

Wherefore take no disdain
At my style rude and plain;
For I rebuke no man
That virtuous is: why then
Wreak ye your anger on me?
For those that virtuous be
Have no cause to say
That I speak out of the way.
Of no good bishop speak I,
Nor good priest I escry,
Good friar, nor good chanon,
Good nun, nor good canon,
Good monk, nor good clerk,
Nor yet of no good work.
But my recounting is
Of them that do amiss,
In speaking and rebelling,
In hindering and disavailing
Holy Church, our mother,
One against another;
To use such despiting
Is all my whole writing;
To hinder no man,
As near as I can,
For no man have I named:
Wherefore should I be blamed?
Ye ought to be ashamed,
Against me to be gramed,
And can tell no cause why,
But that I write truly.
    Then if any there be
Of high or low degree
Of the spiritualty
Or of the temporalty,
That doth think or ween
That his conscience be not clean,
And feeleth himself sick
Or touched on the quick,
Such grace God them send
Themself to amend,

For I will not pretend
Any man to offend. 1130
   Wherefore, as thinketh me,
Great idiots they be,
And little grace they have,
This treatise to deprave;
Nor will hear no preaching,
Nor no virtuous teaching,
Nor will have no reciting
Of any virtuous writing;
Will know none intelligence
To reform their negligence, 1140
But live still out of fashion
To their own damnation.
To do shame they have no shame,
But they would no man should them blame:
They have an evil name,
But yet they will occupy the same.
   With them the word of God
Is counted for no rod;
They count it for a railing,
That nothing is availing; 1150
The preachers with evil hailing:
'Shall they daunt us prelates
That be their primates?
Not so hardy on their pates!
Hark, how the losel prates,
With a wide weasand!
Avaunt, sir Guy of Gaunt!
Avaunt, lewd priest, avaunt!
Avaunt, sir doctor Devyas!
Prate of thy matins and thy mass, 1160
And let our matters pass;
How darest thou, dawcock, mell?
How darest thou, losel,
Allegate the gospel
Against us of the council?
Avaunt to the devil of hell!
Take him, warden of the Fleet,
Set him fast by the feet!

45

I say, lieutenant of the Tower,
Make this lurden for to lour;   1170
Lodge him in Little Ease,
Feed him with beans and pease!
The King's Bench or Marshalsea
Have him thither by and by!
The villain preacheth openly
And declareth our villainy;
And of our fee-simpleness
He says that we are reckless
And full of wilfulness,
Shameless and merciless,   1180
Incorrigible and insatiate;
And after this rate
Against us doth prate.'

.   .   .   .

And so it seemeth they play   1236
Which hate to be corrected
When they be infected,
Nor will suffer this book
By hook ne by crook   1240
Printed for to be,
For that no man should see
Nor read in any scrolls
Of their drunken nolls
Nor of their noddy polls,
Nor of their silly souls,
Nor of some witless pates
Of divers great estates,
As well as other men.
    Now to withdraw my pen   1250
And now awhile to rest
Meseemeth it for the best.
The forecastle of my ship
Shall glide and smoothly slip
Out of the waves wood
Of the stormy flood,
Shoot anchor and lie at road
And sail not far abroad

46

Till the coast be clear
And the lodestar appear.
My ship now will I steer
Towards the *port salut*
Of our saviour Jesu,
Such grace that he us send
To rectify and amend
Things that are amiss
When that his pleasure is.
          Amen!

3 · SIR THOMAS WYATT

My mother's maids, when they did sew and spin,
  They sang sometime a song of the fieldmouse,
  That for because her livelihood was but thin,
Would needs go seek her townish sister's house.
  She thought herself endured to much pain,
  The stormy blasts her cave so sore did souse,
That when the furrows swimmed with the rain
  She must lie cold and wet in sorry plight;
  And worse than that, bare meat there did remain
To comfort her when she her house had dight;   10
  Sometime a barleycorn, sometime a bean,
  For which she laboured hard both day and night,
In harvest-time whilst she might go and glean;
  And when her store was 'stroyed with the flood,
  Then wellaway! for she undone was clean.
Then was she fain to take instead of food
  Sleep if she might, her hunger to beguile.
  'My sister', quoth she, 'hath a living good,
And hence from me she dwelleth not a mile.
  In cold and storm she lieth warm and dry   20
  In bed of down; the dirt doth not defile
Her tender foot. She laboureth not as I.
  Richly she feedeth, and at the rich man's cost,
  And for her meat she needs not crave nor cry.

By sea, by land, of delicates the most
    Her cater seeks and spareth for no peril;
    She feedeth on boiled bacon-meat and roast,
And hath thereof neither charge nor travail;
    And when she list the liquor of the grape
    Doth glad her heart, till that her belly swell.'   30
And at this journey she maketh but a jape;
    So forth she goeth trusting of all this wealth
    With her sister her part so for to shape
That if she might keep herself in health
    To live a lady while her life doth last.
    And to the door now she is come by stealth,
And with her foot anon she scrapeth full fast.
    The other for fear durst not well scarce appear,
    Of every noise so was the wretch aghast.
At last she asked softly who was there,   40
    And in her language as well as she could
    'Pepe', quoth the other sister, 'I am here.'
'Peace', quoth the towny mouse, 'Why speakest thou so loud?'
    And by the hand she took her fair and well.
    'Welcome', quoth she, 'my sister, by the rood!'
She feasted her, that joy it was to tell
    The fare they had; they drank the wine so clear.
    And as to purpose now and then it fell
She cheered her with 'How, sister, what cheer?'
    Amidst this joy befell a sorry chance,   50
    That, wellaway! the stranger bought full dear
The fare she had; for as she looked askance
    Under a stool she spied two steaming eyes
    In a round head with sharp ears. In France
Was never mouse so feared, for though the unwise
    Had not y-seen such a beast before,
    Yet had Nature taught her after her guise
To know her foe and dread him evermore.
    The towny mouse fled, she knew whither to go.
    The other had no shift but wonders sore,   60
Feared of her life: at home she wished her tho,
    And to the door, alas, as she did skip—
    The heaven it would, lo, and eke her chance was so—
At the threshold her silly foot did trip,

48

And ere she might recover it again
The traitor cat had caught her by the hip
And made her there against her will remain,
    That had forgotten her poor surety and rest
    For seeming wealth wherein she thought to reign.

Alas, my Poynz, how men do seek the best,   70
    And find the worst, by error as they stray!
    And no marvel: when sight is so oppressed,
And blind the guide, anon out of the way
    Goeth guide and all in seeking quiet life.
    O wretched minds, there is no gold that may
Grant that ye seek! No war, no peace, no strife;
    No, no, although thy head were hooped with gold,
    Sergeant with mace, halberd, sword nor knife
Cannot repulse the care that follow should.
    Each kind of life hath with him his disease.   80
    Live in delight even as thy lust would,
And thou shalt find when lust doth most thee please
    It irketh straight and by itself doth fade.
    A small thing it is that may thy mind appease.
None of ye all there is that is so mad
    To seek grapes upon brambles or briars,
    Nor none, I trow, that hath his wit so bad
To set his hay for coneys over rivers,
    Ne yet set not a drag-net for an hare;
    And yet the thing that most is your desire   90
Ye do misseek with more travail and care.
    Make plain thine heart that it be not knotted
    With hope or dread, and see thy will be bare
From all affects whom vice hath ever spotted;
    Thyself content with that is thee assigned,
    And use it well that is to thee allotted.
Then seek no more out of thyself to find
    The thing that thou hast sought so long before,
    For thou shalt feel it sitting in thy mind.
Mad, if ye list to continue your sore,   100
    Let present pass and gape on time to come
    And dip yourself in travail more and more.
Henceforth, my Poynz, this shall be all and some:

These wretched fools shall have nought else of me;
    But to the great God and to his high doom
None other pain pray I for them to be
    But when the rage doth lead them from the right
    That looking backwards virtue they may see
Even as she is, so goodly fair and bright;
    And whilst they clasp their lusts in arms across   110
    Grant them, good Lord, as thou mayst of thy might,
    To fret inwards for losing such a loss.

                                    (*Satire II*)

4 · SIR THOMAS WYATT

A spending hand that alway poureth out *a*
    Had need to have a bringer in as fast, *b*
    And on the stone that still doth turn about *a*
There groweth no moss: these proverbs yet do last. *b*
    Reason hath set them in so sure a place *c*
    That length of years their force can never waste. *c*
When I remember this, and eke the case *c*   *c*
    Wherein thou stands, I thought forthwith to write,
    Brian, to thee, who knows how great a grace *c*
In writing is to counsel man the right. *a*   10
    To thee, therefore, that trots still up and down *d*
    And never rests, but running day and night *a*
From realm to realm, from city, street and town, *d*
    Why dost thou wear thy body to the bones, *e* *d*
    And mightest at home sleep in thy bed of down *d*
And drink good ale so nappy for the nonce, *e*
    Feed thy self fat and heap up pound by pound? *f*
    Likest thou not this? 'No.' Why? 'For swine so groins
In sty and chaw the turds moulded on the ground,
    And drivel on pearls, the head still in the manger;   20
    So of the harp the ass doth hear the sound.
So sacks of dirt be filled up in the cloister
    That serves for less than do these fatted swine.
    Though I seem lean and dry without moisture,

Yet will I serve my prince, my lord and thine,
    And let them live to feed the paunch that list,
    So may I feed to live both me and mine.'
By God, well said! But what and if thou wist
    How to bring in as fast as thou dost spend?
    'That would I learn.' And it shall not be missed   30
To tell thee how. Now hark what I intend.
    Thou knowest well first who so can seek to please
    Shall purchase friends where truth shall but offend.
Flee therefore truth: it is both wealth and ease.
    For though that truth of every man hath praise,
    Full near that wind goeth truth in great misease.
Use virtue as it goeth nowadays:
    In word alone to make thy language sweet,
    And of the deed yet do not as thou says;
Else be thou sure thou shalt be far unmeet   40
    To get thy bread, each thing is now so scant.
    Seek still thy profit upon thy bare feet.
Lend in no wise, for fear that thou do want,
    Unless it be as to a dog a cheese:
    By which return be sure to win a cant
Of half at least: it is not good to lese.
    Learn at Kittson, that in a long white coat
    From under the stall without lands or fees
Hath leapt into the shop, who knoweth by rote
    This rule that I have told thee here before.   50
    Sometime also rich age beginneth to dote:
See thou when there thy gain may be the more.
    Stay him by the arm, whereso he walk or go;
    Be near alway; and if he cough too sore,
When he hath spit, tread out and please him so.
    A diligent knave that picks his master's purse
    May please him so that he withouten mo
Executor is: and what is he the worse?
    But if so chance you get nought of the man,
    The widow may for all thy charge deburse.   60
A rivelled skin, a stinking breath, what then?
    A toothless mouth shall do thy lips no harm:
    The gold is good, and though she curse or ban,
Yet where thee list thou mayst lie good and warm;

Let the old mule bite upon the bridle
Whilst there do lie a sweeter in thine arm.
In this also see you be not idle:
    Thy niece, thy cousin, thy sister or thy daughter,
    If she be fair, if handsome be her middle,
If thy better hath her love besought her,   70
    Advance his cause and he shall help thy need.
    It is but love: turn it to a laughter.
But ware, I say, so gold thee help and speed,
    That in this case thou be not so unwise
    As Pandar was in such a like deed;
For he, the fool, of conscience was so nice
    That he no gain would have for all his pain.
    Be next thyself, for friendship bears no price.
Laughst thou at me? Why, do I speak in vain?
    'No, not at thee, but at thy thrifty jest.   80
    Wouldst thou I should for any loss or gain
Change that for gold that I have ta'en for best
    Next godly things—to have an honest name?
    Should I leve that, then take me for a beast!'
Nay then, farewell! And if thou care for shame,
    Content thee then with honest poverty,
    With free tongue what thee mislikes to blame,
And for thy truth sometime adversity:
    And therewithal this thing I shall thee give—
    In this world now little prosperity,   90
And coin to keep as water in a sieve.

(Satire III)

5 · THOMAS DRANT

Horace, Satires, II, i

The poet is at altercation with himself, and reasoneth if he should any further proceed in inditing of satyres, since he was thought of some envious persons to be sharp-spoken, and indeed a backbiter. He demandeth counsel of the lawyer Trebatius; he defendeth his own deed and convinceth his misjudgers.

Horace	Some think my satyre's too too tart
	to keep no constant law,
	And some have thought it loosely penned,
	whatso of mine they saw;
	And ween a thousand suchlike rhymes
	one might within a day
	Write and despatch. Old friend Trebate,
	what should I do? A way
	To me prescribe. You bid me rest,
	my Muses to appal?
Trebatius	—Nay, trust me truly, by my thrift,
	that were the best of all.
Horace	—But I must needs be doing still:
	you bid me, I know not what,
	To swim in Tiber all the day,
	at night to keep a chat;
	To drink for life, to quaff, carouse,
	to load my totty noll,
	And by such means restrain my pen
	and to surcharge my soul.
	Of if I have such urgent lust
	and liking to indite,
	That then I should of Caesar's frays
	and passing triumphs write:
	For that would fetch us in the pence
	and help me for to live.
	Alas, God knows, full fain would I:
	my courage will not give
	Me so to do. Not every man
	the warlike troops so gay

10

20

30

To Moorish pikes and broaching spears,
  the Frenchmen slain in fray,
The puissant Percy plucked from horse,
  praiseworthy can display.
Why might I not, just Scipio,
  thy martial feats have praised
As learned Lucile once tofore
  such bloody banquets blazed?
I will assay, as time shall serve
  (unless I waste my time):   40
It is in vain to exhibit
  to Caesar any rhyme:
whom, if a man attempt to claw,
  inflexible he stands;
yet better were so to presume
  than for to 'file our hands
With bankrupt slave Pantabolus
  and Nomentanus' pranks,
Since causeless all mistrust themselves
  and cons me little thanks.   50
What way for me? they say that I
  am subject unto drink,
And sottishly upon excess
  lay out whatso I think,
Like drunken folk that hop and skip
  when liquor loads their brain,
And when, through ill-affected eye,
  one candle seemeth twain.
Born of one egg, Pollux on foot
  and Castor loves to ride: 60
Each man his mind: in studying
  how many ways be tried.
I keep one stay, of writing (they say)
  in melancholy mood—
Like Lucile, saving that my wit
  is not all-out so good.
Lucile, as to his very friend,
  so would he to his book
His secrets good or bad bewray:
  look on them, who would look.   70

Him follow I: in Lucanie
  or bred in Apulie
I wot not, for Venuse my town
  betwixt them both doth lie.
The Romans Venusine possess,
  so sent into that place
Lest people nigh a-bordering
  might win the town in space
And thereby 'noy the Romish wealth;
  whatso my country is,   80
Whatso my wit, my bitter style
  strikes not a whit amiss.
It may be likened to a sword
  in sheathe for my defence:
Since no false losels hurt me then
  why do I draw it thence?
O king, O father Jupiter,
  would God the times were so
That rust might well devour this sword,
  that none would work me woe.   90
But work they do, but whoso does,
  though he be devilish fell,
A blazon far and near his arms
  and wanton touches tell.
He may go howl and pule for woe,
  the citizens will scorn him
And cause him wish full many a time
  his dam had never born him.
The lawyer, when that he is chased,
  will threaten judgment fell: 100
So Canadie our sorceress
  with poison will us quell;
Each officer doth menace eke
  the worst that they can do:
All brag of that which is their best
  and therewith fear their foe.
And that Nature allows of this
  mark thou these notes with me:
The wolf with tooth, the bull with horn,
  and how this same might be   110

Dame Nature teacheth inwardly.
   Thou dost again reply,
Strong Sheva would not with his sword
   his mother cause to die
Though she had wrought him much mischief.
   No marvel, for the ox
Strikes not with tooth, nor wolf with heel:
   strong poison used this fox.
So he and they, the good and lewd,
   their weapons have by kind   120
And used the same to work their weal;
   the gifts therefore of mind
Shall be my best artillery:
   for whether quiet age
Abideth me, or black-winged death
   encompass me in rage,
Come wealth or want, at home, or else
   perchance an exiled man,
I will not fail to write my state
   if possibly I can.   130
Trebatius —My son, if that thou write so sharp
   no doubt thou shalt not live;
Someone or other will to thee
   thy fatal wound y-give.
Horace   —Why, Lucile lived, who ever used
   all feigners to detect
With satyres sharp, and quippès round:
   of death he never recked.
But blamed those which outwardly
   do give a shining show,   140
And inwardly are charged with sin,
   that uneathes they can go.
Good Lelie did not hate his wit,
   nor he that got renown
For policy, and prowess too,
   for beating Carthage down.
I say they were not miscontent
   that lewd Metellus once
And loutish Lupus were reformed
   with satyres for the nonce.   150

He would not spare the officers
    nor private men to blame;
A friend to none save honesty
    and those that used the same.
With doughty stout duke Scipio
    and Lelie learned and wise
He would jest very jocundly
    and frankly in his guise,
At meals, when he sequestered was
    from the unlettered sort.   160
Whatso I am, though far I wot
    from Lucile's wit and port,
Yet envy's self cannot deny
    but I have led my life
Amongst the best, though some men think
    me dedicate to strife:
Methinks my ground is good and sure;
    except you, friend Trebate,
By law do disallow of it,
    I will pursue my state.   170
Trebatius Beware, beware, the warned may live,
    be circumspect and slow,
Lest you by words undo yourself
    through ignorance of law.
For who that writeth slanderously,
    we lawyers must amend him.
Horace And who that writeth true and well,
    our Caesar must defend him.
If that a man speak of a zeal
    and blame the bad alone,   180
Despatch your rolls: there is no gain;
    the lawyer may be gone.

6 · ANONYMOUS

God send every priest a wife,
    And every nun a man,
That they might live that holy life
    As first the Kirk began.

Saint Peter, whom none can reprove,
    His life in marriage led:
All good priests who God did love
    Their married wivės had.

Great cause, then, I grant, had they,
    From wivės to refrain: 10
But greater causes have they may
    Now wives to wed again.

For then should not so many whore
    Be up and down this land;
Nor yet so many beggars poor
    In kirk and market stand.

And not so mickle bastard seed
    Throughout this country sown;
Nor good men uncouth fry should feed,
    And all the truth were known.   20

Since Christės law, and common law,
    And Doctors will admit,
That priestės in that yoke should draw,
    Who dare say contrair it.

                    (From *Gude and Godlie Ballatis*)

7 · ANONYMOUS

With huntis up, with huntis up,
    It is now perfect day;
Jesus our King is gone in hunting,
    Who likes to speed they may.

A cursed fox lay did in rocks
    This long and many a day,
Devouring sheep while he might creep,
    None might him scare away.

It did him good to lap the blood
  Of young and tender lambs:
None could he miss, for all was his,
  The young ones with their dams.

The hunter is Christ, that hunts in haste,
  The hounds are Peter and Paul,
The Pope is the fox, Rome is the rocks,
  That rubs us on the gall.

That cruel beast, he never ceased,
  By his usurped power,
By his dispense to get our pence
  Our soulès to devour.

Who could devise such merchandise
  As he that there to sell,
Unless it were proud Lucifer
  The great master of Hell.

He had to sell the Tantony bell,
  And pardons therein was;
Remission of sins in old sheepskins,
  Our souls to bring from grace.

With bulls of lead, white wax and red,
  And otherwhiles with green,
Closed in a box, this used the fox,
  Such paltry was never seen.

With dispensations and obligations,
  According to his law,
He would dispense, for money from hence,
  With them he never saw.

To curse and ban the poor simple man,
  That had nought to flee the pain;
But when he had paid it all to a mite,
  He must be absolved then.

To some, God wot, he gave tot quot,
  And other some plurality:
But first with pence he must dispense,
  Or else it will nought be.

59

Kings to marry, and some to tarry,
    Such is his power and might,
Who that has gold, with him will he hold,
    Though it be contrair all right.

O blessed Peter, the fox is a liar,
    Thou knows well it is not so,   50
Till at the last he shall be down cast,
    His paltry, pardons and all.

(From *Gude and Godlie Ballatis*)

8 · GEORGE GASCOIGNE

The Steel Glass

And who desires, at large to know my name,   54
My birth, my line, and every circumstance,
Lo read it here: Plain-dealing was my sire,
And he begat me by Simplicity,
A pair of twins at one self burden born,
My sister and I into this world were sent.
My sister's name was pleasant Poesis,   60
And I myself had Satyra to name,
Whose hap was such, that in the prime of youth,
A lusty lad, a stately man to see,
Brought up in place where pleasures did abound,
(I dare not say in court for both mine ears)
Began to woo my sister, not for wealth,
But for her face was lovely to behold,
And therewithal her speech was pleasant still.
This noble's name was called Vain Delight,
And in his train, he had a comely crew   70
Of guileful wights: False Semblant was the first,
The second man was Flearing Flattery
(Brethren belike, or very near of kin);
Then followed them Detraction and Deceit.
Sym Swash did bear a buckler for the first,
False Witness was the second stemly page;

And thus well-armed, and in good equipage,
This gallant came unto my father's court,
And wooed my sister, for she elder was
And fairer eke, but out of doubt (at least)   80
Her pleasant speech surpassed mine so much
That Vain Delight to her address'd his suit.
    Short tale to make, she gave a free consent,
And forth she goeth to be his wedded make,
Entic'd percase with gloss of gorgeous show,
(Or else perhaps persuaded by his peers)
That constant love had harbour'd in his breast.
Such errors grow where such false prophets preach.
Howso it were, my sister liked him well,
And forth she goeth, in court with him to dwell.   90
Where, when she had some years y-sojourned,
And saw the world, and marked each man's mind,
A deep desire her loving heart inflamed
To see me sit by her in seemly wise,
That company might comfort her sometimes,
And sound advice might ease her weary thoughts;
And forth with speed (even at her first request)
Doth Vain Delight his hasty course direct;
To seek me out his sails are fully bent,
And wind was good to bring me to the bower   100
Whereas she lay, that mourned days and nights
To see herself so match'd and so deceiv'd.
And when the wretch (I cannot term him bet)
Had me on seas full far from friendly help,
A spark of lust did kindle in his breast
And bade him hark to songs of Satyra.
I silly soul (which thought nobody harm)
'Gan clear my throat, and strave to sing my best,
Which pleased him so, and so inflam'd his heart,
That he forgot my sister Poesis   110
And ravished me, to please his wanton mind.
    Not so content, when this foul fact was done,
(Y-fraught with fear, lest that I should disclose
His incest and his doting dark desire)
He caused straightways the foremost of his crew
With his compeer, to try me with their tongues:

And when their guiles could not prevail to win
My simple mind from track of trusty truth,
Nor yet deceit could blear mine eyes through fraud,
Came Slander then, accusing me, and said   120
That I enticed Delight to love and lust.
Thus was I caught, poor wretch that thought none ill.
And furthermore, to cloak their own offence,
They clapped me fast in cage of Misery,
And there I dwelt full many a doleful day
Until this thief, this traitor Vain Delight,
Cut out my tongue, with Razor of Restraint,
Lest I should wray this bloody deed of his.
    And thus (my Lord) I live a weary life,
Not as I seemed, a man sometimes of might,   130
But womanlike, whose tears must 'venge her harms.
And yet, even as the mighty gods did deign
For Philomel, that though her tongue were cut
Yet should she sing a pleasant note sometimes:
So have they deign'd by their divine decrees
That with the stumps of my reproved tongue
I may sometimes reprovers' deeds reprove,
And sing a verse to make them see themselves.

    Then thus I sing this silly song by night,
Like Philomene, since that the shining sun   140
Is now eclips'd, which wont to lend me light.
    And thus I sing, in corner closely couch'd,
Like Philomene, since that the stately courts
Are now no place for such poor birds as I.
    And thus I sing, with prick against my breast,
Like Philomene, since that the privy worm,
Which makes me see my reckless youth misspent,
May well suffice to keep me waking still.
    And thus I sing, when pleasant spring begins,
Like Philomene, since every jangling bird   150
Which squeaketh loud, shall never triumph so,
As though my muse were mute and durst not sing.
    And thus I sing, with harmless true intent,
Like Philomene, when as percase (meanwhile)
The Cuckoo sucks mine eggs by foul deceit,

62

And licks the sweet which might have fed me first.
    And thus I mean in mournful wise to sing
A rare conceit (God grant it like my Lord),
A trusty tune, from ancient cliffs convey'd,
A plain-song note, which cannot warble well.   160

    For whiles I mark this weak and wretched world,
Wherein I see how every kind of man
Can flatter still, and yet deceives himself,
I seem to muse, from whence such error springs,
Such gross conceits, such mists of dark mistake,
Such surquedry, such weening over-well,
And yet, in deed, such dealings too too bad.
And as I stretch my weary wits to weigh
The cause thereof, and whence it should proceed,
My battered brains (which now be shrewdly bruised   170
With cannon-shot of much misgovernment)
Can spy no cause but only one conceit
Which makes me think the world go'th still awry.
    I see and sigh (because it makes me sad)
That peevish pride doth all the world possess,
And every wight will have a looking-glass
To see himself, yet so he seeth him not:
Yea (shall I say?) a glass of common glass
Which glist'reth bright, and shows a seemly show,
Is not enough: the days are past and gone   180
That beryl glass, with foils of lovely brown,
Might serve to show a seemly-favour'd face.
That age is dead and vanish'd long ago
Which thought that steel both trusty was and true,
And needed not a foil of contraries,
But show'd all things even as they were in deed.
Instead whereof, our curious years can find
The crystal glass, which glimseth brave and bright,
And shows the thing much better than it is,
Beguiled with foils, of sundry subtle sights,   190
So that they seem, and covet not to be.
    This is the cause (believe me now my Lord)
That realms do rue from high prosperity,
That kings decline from princely government,

63

That lords do lack their ancestors' good-will,
That knights consume their patrimony still,
That gentlemen do make the merchant rise,
That ploughmen beg, and craftsmen cannot thrive,
That clergy quails and hath small reverence,
That laymen live by moving mischief still,   200
That courtiers thrive at latter Lammas-day,
That officers can scarce enrich their heirs,
That soldiers starve, or preach at Tyburn-cross,
That lawyers buy, and purchase deadly hate,
That merchants climb and fall again as fast,
That roisters brag above their betters' room,
That sycophants are counted jolly guests,
That Lais leads a lady's life aloft,
And Lucrece lurks with sober bashful grace.
    This is the cause (or else my Muse mistakes)   210
That things are thought which never yet were wrought,
And castles built above in lofty skies
Which never yet had good foundation.
And that the same may seem no feigned dream,
But words of worth and worthy to be weigh'd,
I have presum'd my Lord for to present
With this poor glass which is of trusty steel,
And came to me by will and testament
Of one that was a Glassmaker indeed.
    Lucilius this worthy man was nam'd,   220
Who at his death bequeath'd the crystal glass
To such as love to seem but not to be;
And unto those that love to see themselves,
How foul or fair soever that they are,
He 'gan bequeath a glass of trusty steel,
Wherein they may be bold always to look,
Because it shows all things in their degree.
And since myself (now pride of youth is past)
Do love to be, and let all seeming pass,
Since I desire to see myself indeed,   230
Not what I would, but what I am or should,
Therefore I like this trusty glass of steel.

9 · EDMUND SPENSER

Mother Hubberd's Tale

[The Fox and the Ape, lacking advancement, decide to wander through
the world seeking their fortune.]

At last they chanced to meet upon the way   581
The Mule, all decked in goodly rich array,
With bells and bosses that full loudly rung,
And costly trappings that to ground down hung.
Lowly they him saluted in meek wise,
But he through pride and fatness 'gan despise
Their meanness; scarce vouchsafed them to requite.
Whereat the Fox, deep groaning in his sprite,
Said 'Ah, sir Mule, now blessed be the day
That I see you so goodly and so gay   590
In your attires, and eke your silken hide
Filled with round flesh, that every bone doth hide.
Seems that in fruitful pastures ye do live,
Or fortune doth you secret favour give.'
'Foolish Fox' (said the Mule) 'thy wretched need
Praiseth the thing that doth thy sorrow breed.
For well I ween, thou canst not but envy
My wealth, compared to thine own misery,
That art so lean and meagre waxen late
That scarce thy legs uphold thy feeble gait.'   600
'Ay me' (said then the Fox) 'whom evil hap
Unworthy in such wretchedness doth wrap
And makes the scorn of other beasts to be:
But rede (fair Sir, of grace), from whence come ye?
Or what of tidings you abroad do hear?
News may perhaps some good unweeting bear.'
   'From royal court I lately came' (said he)
'Where all the bravery that eye may see
And all the happiness that heart desire
Is to be found; he nothing can admire   610
That hath not seen that heaven's portraiture:
But tidings there is none, I you assure,
Save that which common is and known to all:
That courtiers as the tide do rise and fall.'

'But tell us' (said the Ape) 'we do you pray,
Who now in court doth bear the greatest sway;
That if such fortune do to us befall
We may seek favour of the best of all.'
'Marry' (said he) 'the highest now in grace
Be the wild beasts, that swiftest are in chase;   620
For in their speedy course and nimble flight
The Lion now doth take the most delight:
But chiefly joys on foot them to behold
Enchased with chain and circulet of gold;
So wild a beast so tame y-taught to be
And buxom to his bands, is joy to see.
So well his golden circlet him beseemeth:
But his late chain his liege unmeet esteemeth;
For so brave beasts she loveth best to see
In the wild forest ranging fresh and free.   630
Therefore if fortune thee in court to live,
In case thou ever there wilt hope to thrive,
To some of these thou must thyself apply:
Else, as a thistledown in th'air doth fly,
So vainly shalt thou to and fro be tossed
And lose thy labour and thy fruitless cost.
And yet full few, which follow them I see,
For virtue's bare regard advanced be:
But either for some gainful benefit,
Or that they may for their own turns be fit.   640
Nathless perhaps ye things may handle so
That ye may better thrive than thousands mo.'
   'But' (said the Ape) 'how shall we first come in,
That after we may favour seek to win?'
'How else' (said he) 'but with a good bold face
And with big words and with a stately pace,
That men may think of you in general,
That to be in you which is not at all:
For not by that which is the world now deemeth
(As it was wont) but by that same that seemeth.   650
Ne do I doubt, but that ye well can fashion
Yourselves thereto, according to occasion:
So fare ye well; good courtiers may ye be.'
So proudly neighing from them parted he.

66

Then 'gan this crafty couple to devise
How for the court themselves they might aguise:
For thither they themselves meant to address
In hope to find there happier success;
So well they shifted, that the Ape anon
Himself had clothed like a gentleman,   660
And the sly Fox as like to be his groom,
That to the court in seemly sort they come:
Where the fond Ape himself uprearing high
Upon his tiptoes, stalketh stately by
As if he were some great Magnifico,
And boldly doth among the boldest go.
And his man Reynold with fine counterfeisance
Supports his credit and his countenance.
Then 'gan the courtiers gaze on every side
And stare on him, with big looks basin-wide,   670
Wondering what mister wight he was, and whence:
For he was clad in strange accoutrements,
Fashioned with quaint devices never seen
In court before, yet there all fashions been;
Yet he them in newfangleness did pass.
But his behaviour altogether was
Alla Turchesca, much the more admired,
And his looks lofty, as if he aspired
To dignity, and 'sdained the low degree;
That all which did such strangeness in him see   680
By secret means 'gan of his state enquire,
And privily his servant thereto hire:
Who throughly armed against such coverture
Reported unto all, that he was sure
A noble gentleman of high regard
Which through the world had with long travel fared,
And seen the manners of all beasts on ground;
Now here arrived, to see if like he found.
    Thus did the Ape at first him credit gain,
Which afterwards he wisely did maintain   690
With gallant show, and daily more augment
Through his fine feats and courtly complement;
For he could play, and dance, and vault, and spring,
And all that else pertains to revelling,

67

Only through kindly aptness of his joints.
Besides, he could do many other points,
The which in court him served to good stead:
For he 'mongst ladies could their fortunes read
Out of their hands, and merry leasings tell,
And juggle finely, that became him well: 700
But he so light was at legerdemain
That what he touched came not to light again;
Yet would he laugh it out, and proudly look,
And tell them that they greatly him mistook.
So would he scoff them out with mockery,
For he therein had great felicity;
And with sharp quips 'joyed others to deface,
Thinking that their disgracing did him grace:
So whilst that other like vain wits he pleased,
And made to laugh, his heart was greatly eased.   710
   But the right gentle mind would bite his lip,
To hear the javel so good men to nip:
For though the vulgar yield an open ear
And common courtiers love to gibe and fleer
At everything which they hear spoken ill,
And the best speeches with ill-meaning spill;
Yet the brave courtier, in whose beauteous thought
Regard of honour harbours more than aught,
Doth loathe such base condition, to backbite
Any's good name for envy or despite.   720
He stands on terms of honourable mind,
Ne will be carried with the common wind
Of courts' inconstant mutability,
Ne after every tattling fable fly;
But hears and sees the follies of the rest,
And thereof gathers for himself the best:
He will not creep, nor crouch with feigned face,
But walks upright with comely steadfast pace,
And unto all doth yield due courtesy:
But not with kissed hand below the knee   730
As that same apish crew is wont to do:
For he disdains himself to embase thereto.
He hates foul leasings and vile flattery,
Two filthy blots in noble gentry,

And loathful idleness he doth detest,
The canker worm of every gentle breast;
The which to banish, with fair exercise
Of knightly feats he daily doth devise:
Now managing the mouths of stubborn steeds,
Now practising the proof of warlike deeds, 740
Now his bright arms assaying, now his spear,
Now the nigh-aimed ring away to bear.
At other times he casts to sue the chase
Of swift wild beasts, or run on foot a race
To enlarge his breath (large breath in arms most needful)
Or else by wrestling to wax strong and heedful;
Or his stiff arms to stretch with yewghen bow,
And manly legs, still passing to and fro
Without a gowned beast him fast beside,
A vain ensample of the Persian pride, 750
Who after he had won th' Assyrian foe
Did ever after scorn on foot to go.
Thus when this courtly gentleman with toil
Himself hath wearied, he doth recoil
Unto his rest, and there with sweet delight
Of music's skill revives his toiled sprite,
Or else with loves, and ladies' gentle sports,
The joy of youth, himself he recomforts;
Or lastly, when the body list to pause,
His mind unto the Muses he withdraws: 760
Sweet lady Muses, ladies of delight,
Delights of life and ornaments of light:
With whom he close confers with wise discourse
Of Nature's works, of heaven's continual course,
Of foreign lands, of people different,
Of kingdoms' change, of divers government,
Of dreadful battles of renowned knights,
With which he kindleth his ambitious sprites
To like desire and praise of noble fame,
The only upshot whereto he doth aim. 770
For all his mind on honour fixed is
To which he levels all his purposes,
And in his Prince's service spends his days
Not so much for to gain, or for to raise

Himself to high degree, as for his grace,
And in his liking to win worthy place,
Through due deserts and comely carriage,
In whatso please employ his personage,
That may be matter meet to gain him praise;
For he is fit to use in all assays,   780
Whether for arms and warlike amenance,
Or else for wise and civil governance.
For he is practised well in policy,
And thereto doth his courting most apply:
To learn the interdeal of princes strange,
To mark the intent of councils, and the change
Of states, and eke of private men somewhile,
Supplanted by fine falsehood and fair guile;
Of all the which he gathereth what is fit
To enrich the storehouse of his powerful wit,   790
Which through wise speeches and grave conference
He daily ekes, and brings to excellence.
   Such is the rightfull courtier in his kind:
But unto such the Ape lent not his mind.
Such were for him no fit companions:
Such would descry his lewd conditions.
But the young lusty gallants he did choose
To follow, meet to whom he might disclose
His witless pleasance and ill-pleasing vein.
A thousand ways he them could entertain   800
With all the thriftless games that may be found:
With mumming and with masking all around,
With dice, with cards, with billiards far unfit,
With shuttlecocks, misseeming manly wit,
With courtesans and costly riotize,
Whereof still somewhat to his share did rise:
Ne, them to pleasure, would he sometimes scorn
A Pandar's coat (so basely was he born);
Thereto he could fine loving verses frame
And play the poet oft. But ah, for shame,   810
Let not sweet poets' praise, whose only pride
Is virtue to advance and vice deride,
Be with the work of losels' wit defamed,
Ne let such verses poetry be named.

Yet he the name on him would rashly take,
Maugre the sacred muses, and it make
A servant to the vile affection
Of such as he depended most upon,
And with the sugary sweet thereof allure
Chaste ladies' ears to fantasies impure.   820
To such delights the noble wits he led
Which him relieved, and their vain humours fed
With fruitless follies and unsound delights.
But if perhaps into their noble sprites
Desire of honour or brave thought of arms
Did ever creep, then with his wicked charms
And strong conceits he would it drive away,
Ne suffer it to house there half a day.
And whenso love of letters did inspire
Their gentle wits, and kindly wise desire   830
That chiefly doth each noble mind adorn,
Then he would scoff at learning, and eke scorn
The sectaries thereof, as people base
And simple men, which never came in place
Of world's affairs, but in dark corner mewed,
Muttered of matters, as their books them shewed;
Ne other knowledge ever did attain,
But with their gowns their gravity maintain.
From them he would his impudent lewd speech
Against God's holy ministers oft reach,   840
And mock divines and their profession.
What else then did he by progression
But mock high God himself, whom they profess?
But what cared he for God, or godliness?
All his care was himself how to advance,
And to uphold his courtly countenance
By all the cunning means he could devise,
Were it by honest ways or otherwise
He made small choice: yet sure his honesty
Got him small gains: but shameless flattery,   850
And filthy brocage, and unseemly shifts,
And borrow base, and some good ladies' gifts.
But the best help, which chiefly him sustained,
Was his man Reynold's purchase which he gained.

For he was schooled by kind in all the skill
Of close conveyance, and each practice ill
Of cozenage and cleanly knavery
Which oft maintained his master's bravery.
Besides he used another slippery sleight
In taking on himself in common sight   860
False personages, fit for every stead,
With which he thousands cleanly cozened:
Now like a merchant, merchants to deceive,
With whom his credit he did often leave
In gage, for his gay master's hopeless debt;
Now like a lawyer, when he land would let,
Or sell fee-simples in his master's name
Which he had never, nor aught like the same;
Then would he be a broker and draw in
Both wares and money, by exchange to win;   870
Then would he seem a farmer, that would sell
Bargains of woods, which he did lately fell,
Or corn or cattle, or such other ware,
Thereby to cozen men not well aware.
Of all the which there came a secret fee
To the Ape, that he his countenance might be.
    Besides all this, he used oft to beguile
Poor suitors, that in court did haunt some while:
For he would learn their business secretly,
And then inform his master hastily,   880
That he by means might cast them to prevent
And beg the suit, the which the other meant.
Or otherwise false Reynold would abuse
The simple suitor, and wish him to choose
His master, being one of great regard
In court, to compass any suit not hard
In case his pains were recompensed with reason:
So would he work the silly man by treason
To buy his master's frivolous goodwill,
That had not power to do him good or ill: 890
So pitiful a thing is suitor's state.
    Most miserable man, whom wicked fate
Hath brought to court, to sue for had y-wist,
That few have found, and many one hath missed.

72

Full little knowest thou that hast not tried,
What hell it is, in suing long to bide:
To lose good days that might be better spent;
To waste long nights in pensive discontent;
To speed today, to be put back tomorrow;
To feed on hope, to pine with fear and sorrow;   900
To have thy Prince's grace, yet want her peer's;
To have thy asking, yet wait many years;
To fret thy soul with crosses and with cares;
To eat thy heart through comfortless despairs;
To fawn, to crouch, to wait, to ride, to run,
To spend, to give, to want, to be undone.
Unhappy wight, born to disastrous end,
That doth his life in so long tendance spend.
    Who ever leaves sweet home, where mean estate
In safe assurance, without strife or hate,   910
Finds all things needful for contentment meek,
And will to court, for shadows vain to seek
Or hope to gain, himself will a daw try:
That curse God send unto mine enemy.
For none but such as this bold Ape unblest
Can ever thrive in that unlucky quest;
Or such as hath a Reynold to his man
That by his shifts his master furnish can.
But yet this Fox could not so closely hide
His crafty feats, but that they were descried   920
At length, by such as sat in justice' seat,
Who for the same him foully did entreat;
And having worthily him punished
Out of the court for ever banished.
    And now the Ape, wanting his huckster-man,
That wont provide his necessaries, 'gan
To grow into great lack, ne could uphold
His countenance in those his garments old;
Ne new ones could he easily provide
Though all men him uncased 'gan deride,   930
Like as a puppet placed in a play
Whose part once past all men bid take away:
So that he driven was to great distress
And shortly brought to hopeless wretchedness.

73

Then closely as he might, he cast to leave
The court, not asking any pass or leave;
But ran away in his rent rags by night,
Ne ever stayed in place ne spoke to wight
Till that the Fox his copesmate he had found,
To whom complaining his unhappy stound   940
At last again with him in travel joined,
And with him fared some better chance to find.

10 · EDMUND SPENSER

Colin Clout's Come Home Again

[The poet, in the 'persona' of the 'shepherd' Colin Clout, has been praising
the Queen, and is asked why, having found such grace at court, he has
nevertheless returned to exile in Ireland.]

. . . 'Why, Colin, since thou found'st such grace   652
With Cynthia and all her noble crew,
Why didst thou ever leave that happy place
In which such wealth might unto thee accrue?
And back returnedst to this barren soil,
Where cold and care and penury do dwell,
Here to keep sheep with hunger and with toil?
Most wretched he, that is and cannot tell.'
    'Happy indeed' (said Colin) 'I him hold,   660
That may that blessed presence still enjoy,
Of fortune and of envy uncontrolled,
Which still are wont most happy states to annoy.
But I, by that which little while I proved,
Some part of these enormities did see,
The which in court continually hoved
And followed those which happy seemed to be.
Therefore I, silly man, whose former days
Had in rude fields been altogether spent,
Durst not adventure such unknown ways,   670
Nor trust the guile of fortune's blandishment;
But rather chose back to my sheep to turn,
Whose utmost hardness I before had tried,

Than, having learned repentance late, to mourn
Amongst those wretches which I there descried.'
  'Shepherd' (said Thestylis) 'it seems of spite
Thou speakest thus 'gainst their felicity
Which thou enviest, rather than of right
That aught in them blameworthy thou dost spy.'
  'Cause have I none' (quoth he) 'of cankered will   680
To quite them ill, that me demeaned so well:
But self-regard of private good or ill
Moves me of each, so as I found, to tell;
And eke to warn young shepherds' wandering wit,
Which through report of that life's painted bliss
Abandon quiet home to seek for it,
And leave their lambs to loss, misled amiss.
  For sooth to say, it is no sort of life
For shepherd fit to lead in that same place
Where each one seeks with malice and with strife   690
To thrust down other into foul disgrace
Himself to raise: and he doth soonest rise
That best can handle his deceitful wit
In subtle shifts, and finest sleights devise:
Either by slandering his well-deemed name
Through leasings lewd, and feigned forgery,
Or else by breeding him some blot of blame
By creeping close into his secrecy:
To which him needs a guileful hollow heart
Masked with fair dissembling courtesy,   700
A filed tongue furnished with terms of art,
No art of school, but courtiers' schoolery.
For arts of school have there small countenance,
Counted but toys to busy idle brains;
And there professors find small maintenance
But to be instruments of others' gains.
  Ne is there place for any gentle wit
Unless to please, itself it can apply:
But shouldered is, or out of doors quite shut
As base or blunt, unmeet for melody.   710
For each man's worth is measured by his weed,
As harts by horns or asses by their ears:
Yet asses been not all whose ears exceed,

75

Nor yet all harts, that horns the highest bears.
For highest looks have not the highest mind,
Nor haughty words most full of highest thoughts:
But are like bladders blowen up with wind
That being pricked do vanish into naughts.
Even such is all their vaunted vanity,
Naught else but smoke, that fumeth soon away.   720
Such is their glory that in simple eye
Seem greatest, when their garments are most gay.
So they themselves for praise of fools do sell
And all their wealth for painting on a wall;
With price whereof they buy a golden bell
And purchase highest rooms in bower and hall:
While single truth and simple honesty
Do wander up and down despised of all:
Their plain attire such glorious gallantry
Disdains so much, that none them in doth call.'   730
    'Ah Colin' (then said Hobbinol) 'the blame
Which thou imputest is too general,
As if not any gentle wit of name
Nor honest mind might there be found at all.
For well I wot, sith I myself was there
To wait on Lobbin (Lobbin well thou knewest),
Full many worthy ones then waiting were
As ever else in Prince's court thou viewest.
Of which, among you many yet remain
Whose names I cannot readily now guess: 740
Those that poor suitors' papers do retain
And those that skill of medicine profess.
And those that do to Cynthia expound
The ledden of strange languages in charge:
For Cynthia doth in sciences abound
And gives to their professors stipends large.
Therefore unjustly thou dost wite them all
For that which thou mislikedst in a few.'
    'Blame is' (quoth he) 'more blameless general
Than that which private errors doth pursue: 750
For well I wot that there amongst them be
Full many persons of right worthy parts,
Both for report of spotless honesty

And for profession of all learned arts,
Whose praise hereby no whit impaired is,
Though blame do light on those that faulty be:
For all the rest do most-what fare amiss,
And yet there own misfaring will not see:
For either they be puffed up with pride
Or fraught with envy that their galls do swell,   760
Or they their days to idleness divide,
Or drownded lie in pleasure's wasteful well,
In which like moldwarps nuzzling still they lurk,
Unmindful of chief parts of manliness,
And do themselves, for want of other work,
Vain votaries of lazy love profess,
Whose service high so basely they ensue
That Cupid's self of them ashamed is,
And mustering all his men in Venus' view
Denies them quite for servitors of his.'   770
   'And is love then' (said Corylas) 'once known
In court, and his sweet lore professed there?
I weened sure he was our god alone,
And only wonned in fields and forests here.'
   'Not so' (quoth he) 'love most aboundeth there.
For all the walls and windows there are writ
All full of love, and love, and love my dear,
And all their talk and study is of it.
Ne any there doth brave or valiant seem
Unless that some gay mistress' badge he bears: 780
Ne anyone himself doth aught esteem
Unless he swim in love up to the ears.
But they of love and of his sacred lere
(As it should be) all otherwise devise
Than we poor shepherds are accustomed here,
And him do sue and serve all otherwise.
For with lewd speeches and licentious deeds
His mighty mysteries they do profane,
And use his idle name to other needs,
But as a compliment for courting vain.   790

Good Lord, what a wicked world is this,
  When every man doth live amiss,
And no regard of conscience is,
  And surely the more is the pity.
Amend, therefore, good people all,
  Go speedily for mercy call,
That God may bless both great and small
  In every town and city.

Few men do fear the Lord of might,
  And who regards his word aright,   10
They come to church but for a sight,
  And surely the more is the pity.
Amend, &c.

Pride doth bear so great a sway,
  No man but monsters go by the way,
Dressing themselves in foolish array,
  And surely the more is the pity.
Amend, &c.

Wantonness walks in every place
  That modesty dare not show his face: 20
Discretion counted a fool in this case,
  And surely the more is the pity.
Amend, &c.

Flattery is friended gallantly,
  And bears his countenance very high,
Whose lips are taught to cog and lie,
  And surely the more is the pity.
Amend, &c.

Plain truth is driven out of town,
  And flattery flourisheth in renown,   30
Deceit doth walk in a guarded gown,
  And surely the more is the pity.
Amend, &c.

Cruelty creeps in every place,
    Hatred bears a friendly face,
And slander seeks his neighbour's disgrace,
    And surely the more is the pity.
Amend, &c.

Idleness walks in every coast,
    Yet flaunts it in bravery with the most,   40
Which keepeth Tyburn as hot as a toast,
    And surely the more is the pity.
Amend, &c.

Correction lieth sick in a sweat,
    And wanton children must not be beat,
They will be wilful when they be great:
    And surely the more is the pity.
Amend, &c.

Whoredom is counted a youthful sport,   50
    Greatly pleasing the lecherous sort,
Not caring whither their souls shall resort,
    And surely the more is the pity.
Amend, &c.

The gaming-houses who will shun,
    When tripping dice do daily run,
Till all their wealth from them be won?
    And surely the more is the pity.
Amend, &c.

And few will learn in reason's school
    Which way they may their vices cool,   60
But calls good counsel doting fool,
    And surely the more is the pity.
Amend, &c.

Usury wears a velvet coat,
    By cutting of his brother's throat,
Which without gains will not lend a groat,
    And surely the more is the pity.
Amend, &c.

79

The landlord with his incomes great
  Doth set his house in such a heat   70
The tenant is driven to lie in the street,
  And surely the more is the pity.
Amend, &c.

Covetousness hath taken such root,
  To call and cry there is no boot:
Although the needy die at their foot,
  And surely the more is the pity.
Amend, &c.

Charity now is choked with care,
  Pity is caught in cruelty's snare,   80
And mercy exiled both naked and bare,
  And surely the more is the pity.
Amend, &c.

The father being of greedy kind
  Doth force his daughter against her mind
To marry where she may substance find,
  And surely the more is the pity.
Amend, &c.

What life is led between them twain,
  When one the other doth disdain?   90
Their end must needs be grief and pain,
  And surely the more is the pity.
Amend, &c.

But laying all these things away,
  Remember well your dying day,
And how you shall consume to clay,
  If you be wise and witty.
Amend, &c.
          (*Broadside Ballad: The abuses of this wicked world*)

Truth's Complaint over England

My mournful Muse Melpomene, draw near,
  Thou saddest lady of the sisters three,
And let her plaints in paper now appear
  Whose tears like Ocean billows seem to be:
  And should I note the plaintiff's name to thee?
Men call her Truth: once had in great request,
But banished now of late for craft's behest.

Amidst the rest that set their pen to book,
  She picked me out to tell this woeful tale:
A simple poet, on whose works to look
  The finest heads would think it very stale: 10
  Yet, though unworthy, to my friends' avail
I take the toil, and pray my Muse's aid
To blazon out the tale of Truth dismayed.

Such time as Phoebus from the coloured sky
  Did headlong drive his horses toward the west,
To suffer horned Luna for to pry
  Amidst the dusky dark, new raised from rest,
  As I in fragrant fields with woes oppressed
'Gan walk to drive out melancholy grief,   20
Which in my heart at that time had the chief—

It was my hap fast by a river's side
  To hear a rueful voice lamenting thus:
'You julling streams, even as your waves divide,
  So breaks my heart with passions perilous
  Which fain I would unto the world discuss,
Were any here for to recount my moan,
Whose woeful heart for inward grief doth groan.'

Which said, she cast her dewed eyes askance,
  And spying me, 'gan rouse her heavy head,   30
And prayed me pen her sad and heavy chance
  And she recounted it that present stead.
  I did agree, and granting Truth me fed
With these reports, which I set down in verse,
Which grieves my Muse for sorrows to rehearse.

'Whilom (dear friend) it was my chance to dwell
   Within an island compassed with the wave,
A safe defence a foreign foe to quell:
   Once Albion called, next Britain Brutus gave,
   Now England hight, a plot of beauty brave,   40
Which only soil should seem the seat to be
Of Paradise, if it from sin were free.

Within this place, within this sacred plot,
   I first did frame my first contented bower;
There found I peace and plenty for to float;
   There justice ruled and shined in every stour;
   There was I loved, and sought too, every hour;
Their prince content with plainness loved Truth,
And pride by abstinence was kept from youth.

Then flew not fashions every day from France;   50
   Then sought not nobles novels from afar;
Then land was kept, not hazarded by chance;
   Then quiet mind preserved the soil from jar;
   Cloth kept out cold, the poor relieved were.
This was the state, this was the lucky stour,
While Truth in England kept her stately bower.

Justice did never look with partial eyes;
   Demosthenes was never dumb for gold;
The prince's ears were ope to peasants' cries,
   And false suspect was charely kept in hold;   60
   Religion flourished, livings were not sold
For lucre then, but given by desert,
And each received, and preached with zealous heart.

Then learning was the lodestone of the land,
   Then husbandman was free from shifts of law,
Then faithful promise stood instead of band,
   The drones from busy bee no mel could draw;
   Then love, not fear, did keep the state in awe:
Then, then, did flourish that renowned time
When earth and ashes thrusted not to climb.   70

For as the horse well-manned abides the bit
   And learns his stop by rein in rider's hand,
Where mountain colt that was not saddled yet

82

Runs headlong on amidst the fallowed land,
  Whose fierce resist scarce bends with any band:
So men reclaimed by virtue tread aright,
Where led by follies mischiefs on them light.

Use, masters all, use nurtureth mortal ways;
  Use, use of good, continues happy state;
Use, use of me, made England then have praise;   80
  But since abuse hath banished me of late.
  Alas the while, there runs another rate,
Which while by sad insight I look into,
I see the want of those that have to do.

And yet I see not Sodom: some are good,
  Whose inward bowels daily melt in moan
To see how Britain now is raging wood,
  Hard-hearted, flinty-minded, all in one,
  Bent to abuse and leaving me alone.
Alonely led with careless show of peace,   90
Whereas secure regard doth sin increase.

Some, some there be whom zeal hath swallowed up:
  First, blessed prince, of whom I find relief,
Some noble peers that taste not error's cup,
  Some goodly prelates in the Church are chief.
  Some lawyers led by zeal, lament my grief,
Some merchants follow God, not swallow gold;
Some country swains love Truth, you may be bold.

Yet as great store of darnel mars the seed,
  Which else would spring within a fertile field: 100
And as the fruitful bud is choked by weed,
  Which otherwise a gladsome grape would yield;
  So sometimes wicked men do overwield
And keep in covert those who would direct
The common state, which error doth infect.

Yet Truth must never alter from his name,
  Good prince, said I, ye good; what of herself?
And that is good for princes that do frame
  Themselves to private good, do subjects good;
  Yet that's not that same goodness I would name: 110

83

Good prince, good people, that's the good I crave;
Of princes' goods that goodness would I have.

For as the great commander of the tides,
  God Neptune, can allay the swelling seas,
And make the billows mount on either sides,
  When wandering keels his choler would displease:
  So princes may stir up and soon appease
The commons' heart to do, and to destroy,
That which is good, or this, which threats annoy.

For common state can never sway amiss   120
  When princes' lives do level all aright;
Be it for prince that England happy is,
  Yet hapless England if the fortune light,
  That with the prince the subject seek not right;
Unhappy state, unhappy times they be,
When princes' lives and subjects' disagree.

I know not, I, whence come these wayward woes,
  Whose sudden shows portend this sudden change,
Yet doth misdoubt such sudden fears disclose
  As Truth this present doubts the sequel strange: 130
  When stable head lets stayless members range,
I fear me; as the buildings trust to sand,
So every blast will 'stroy with turn of hand.

When as in court by proud contempt I see
  A fashion feeds the fancies nowadays;
When as in court promotions passed be
  By self-opinion, oft the wise man says
  The turns are strange, and favour soon decays;
And those whom fortune windeth now afloat
By change of favour soon may change their coat.   140

When as election doth but pass by sense,
  Then must I deem the world is fed by shows:
When garish beauty causeth vain expense,
  It seems the man should see, but little knows,
  Repentance is the fruit by loving grows:
So when in court naught but such pleasures be,
Repentance must ensue—we well may see.

But leaving court, where though the bramble grows
  Yet zealous care there sets herself I see,
I do in court but now complain of those
  Who practice that that fits not their degree:
  Whose veins by power full oft corrected be:
But now such colours cloak each bad pretence,
That shows do hold the wise in some suspense.

But I, poor I, though grieved at courtlike scapes,
  Lamenting there the lavish vain expense,
Have farther cause abroad to note escapes
  Where craft doth keep true meaning in suspense:
  And wily worldlings cover their pretence
With holy shapes, and in a holy coat
Doth flattery praise those men that swim afloat.

In nobles' trains who sees not strange misdeems,
  Where each doth gape and catch at private gain,
And fleece the lord, who though he blindfold seems
  By oft attempts doth bar them of their veins;
  The painful wretch who toils with often pains,
He hath fair words, when flattery sucks the sweet:
Thus shows take place, and Truth's trod underfeet.

In England gifts can compass each reproof:
  The bad for gold may soon be counted good,
The wicked gainer for the state's behoof,
  The blindest buzzard to give heavenly food;
  The faintest heart in warlik'st place hath stood:
And who gives most, hath now most store of farms,
Racked rents, the lord with golden fuel warms.

And Justice sore I fear by power is led,
  The poor may cry, and gladly creep to cross,
The rich with wealth, the wealthy now, are fed,
  The simple man now only bears the loss,
  The lawyer he the golden crowns doth toss,
And now hath fees at will with cap and knee,
And each man cries "Good sir, come plead for me".

O sweet the time, when neither folly might
  Mislead your hopes, nor alter old decrees.
O happy Truth when as with sweet delight

150

160

170

180

85

She laboured still for conscience, not for fees.
O blessed time, when zeal with bended knees
'Gan bless the heavens, that bent their powers divine,
The English hearts to wisdom to incline.

But now refused, disdained and set at naught,   190
   Enforced to seek for rest in place unknown,
I wail, poor wretch, that no redress is sought:
   But well I wot, my griefs are not mine own;
   Some bear a part and help to wail my moan:
But all in vain; such colours now are made
That those would mend the miss do dance in shade.'

This said, bewetting all the place with tears,
   And from her eyes expelling floods of moan,
Her lovely locks bespread about her ears,
   She waved her wings, as willing to be gone: 200
   And after pause, she soared away anon,
And thus she said: 'You islanders, adieu,
You banished me before I fled from you.'

L'Envoy. Believe me, countrymen, this thing is true.

13 · THOMAS LODGE

The Discontented Satyre

Such time as from her mother's tender lap
The night arose, guarded with gentle winds:
And with her precious dew refreshed the sap
Of bloom and bark (whilst that her mantle blinds
   The veil of heaven) and every bird was still
   Save Philomel, that did bemoan her ill.

When in the west Orion lift aloft
His starry crest and smiled upon the Twins;
And Cynthia seemly bright (whose eye full oft
Had watched her love) with radiant light begins   10
   To pierce the veil of silence with her beams,
   Sporting with wanton clear on Ocean streams.

86

When little winds in beating of their wings
Did woo the eyes to leave their wonted wake,
And all was hushed save Zephyrus, that sings
With lovely breathings for the sea-nymph's sake:
 My watchful griefs perplext my mind so sore,
 That forth I walked my sorrows to deplore.

The doly season that resembled well
My drooping heart, gave life to my lament:
Each twinkling lamp that in the heavens did dwell
'Gan rest his course to hearken mine intent:
 Forth went I still devising on my fear,
 Distinguishing each footstep with a tear.

My working thought, deluding of my pace,
At last did bring me to a desert dale
(By envious mountains robbed of Phoebus' face)
Where grows no herb to taste of dew's avail:
 In midst thereof, upon a bed of moss,
 A Satyre did his restless body toss.

Stern were his looks, afflicting all the fields
That were in view; his bushy locks undressed
With terror hang, his haviour horror yields,
And with the sight my sorrows were suppressed;
 So near I drew, when suddenly he rose,
 And thus in terms his purpose did disclose.

'Blush, day's eternal lamp, to see thy lot,
Since that thy clear with cloudy darks is scarred;
Lower on, fair Cynthia, for I like thee not;
For borrowed beauties merit no regard:
 Boast, discontent, naught may depress thy power,
 Since in thyself all grief thou dost devour.

Thou art the God whom I alone adore,
Whose power includeth discords all in one;
Confusions are thy food and fatal store;
Thy name is feared where thou art most unknown;
 Thy grace is great, for fortune's laugh and lower
 Assails them not that glory in thy power.

20

30

40

The mind through thee divines on endless things,
And forms a Heaven through others' fond mislikes;
Time loathes thy haunt, yet lends thee many wings:
Refined wits against thy bulwark strikes:
    And when their curious thoughts are overpast,
    They scorn thy books and like thy bent at last.

For who but thou can yield them any gain?
Deprive the world of perfect discontent,
All glories end, true honour straight is slain,
And life itself in error's course is spent,
    All toil doth sort but to a sorry end:
    For through mislikes each learns for to commend.   60

What made fierce Philip's son to manage arms,
To vail the pride of Persia by his sword,
But thou, my God?—that he by others' harms
Might raise his seat, and thereby still afford
    A cause of discontent to them that lost,
    And hate in him that by their power was crossed.

Let envy cease, what prince can make it known
How dear he loves his best-esteemed friends?
For were not some of purpose overthrown,
Who may discern whereto true favour tends?   70
    Thus Princes' discontent doth honour some,
    And others through their hates to credit come.

Without thy help the soldier shuns the field.
You studious arts, how fatal haps had you
If discontents did not some succours yield?
Oh fleeting Fame, who could thy grace pursue,
    Did not my God send emulations out
    To whet the wits and pens of Pallas' rout?

How could the heavens have retrograde aspects
Without thy help? How might the planets find   80
Their oppositions, and their strange effects,
Unless thy power assisted every kind?
    The air by thee at first invented voice,
    Which, once reverberate, straight yields a noise.

The pencil-man, that with a careless hand
Hath shadowed Venus, hates his slack regard;
And all amazed doth discontented stand
And mends the same, that he before had marred.
   Who sees not then, that it was discontent
    That sight to eye and perfect judgment lent?   90

The schoolman that with heedless flourish writes,
Refines his fault, if thou direct his eye:
And then again with wonder he indites
Such sweet sententious lines as never die:
   Lost in myself in praising of thy might,
    My speech yields up his office to delight.'

This said, he smiled, and on his restless bed
Reposed and tossed his indisposed limbs:
A world of thoughts still hammered in his head;
Now would he sleep, and straight his couch he trims: 100
   And then he walks, and therewith sits him down,
    And feigns to sing, yet endeth with a frown.

I stood amazed and wondered at his words,
And sought to suck the soul from out his lips,
His rare discourse such wondrous joy affords:
But unawares, like lightfoot Faun he trips
   Along the lawns: and I, with watch forespent,
    Drew home, and vowed to honour discontent.   108

14 · THOMAS LODGE

In Commendation of a Solitary Life

Not yet forsaken (gentle Muse) draw near,
And help to weary out these worldly thoughts:
Go fit thy method to my moody cheer,
For why? fond pleasure now prevaileth naughts.
   Since when content and wealthy state declines,
    The heart doth droop, and doleful be the lines.

Forthy (fond man) why rest I not at last?
My wings of hope are clipped by foul disgrace:
The silver down of age now flocketh fast,
Like moss on oak to dwell upon my face:
    And what with thought and time, through want and ruth,
    I challenge care for joy, and age for youth.

What fruits of former labours do I find?
My studious pen doth traffic for a scorn;
My due deserts are but repaid with wind,
And what I earn is nought but bitter mourn:
    In which accompt I reap but this advice,
    To cease to climb and live contented-wise.

But gentle Muse, where bodeth this content?
The prince's court is fraught with endless woes;
Corruptions flock where honours do frequent,
The cities swarm with plagues, with suits, with foes:
    High-climbing wits do catch a sudden fall;
    With none of these content list dwell withal.

Ah, beauty of the double-topped hill,
Thou saddest sister of the sacred nine,
What fruitful pleasance followeth now my quill?
What wondrous beauties bless my drooping eyen?
    Even such as erst the shepherd in the shade
    Beheld, when he a poet once was made.

Methinks I see the deserts fresh-arrayed,
New-mantled in their liveries of green,
Whose frolic pride makes smiling heaven apaid,
Wherein the nymphs do weary out their teen,
    Washing their ivory in those murmuring springs
    At whose kind fall the bird with pleasure sings.

See where the babes of Memory are laid
Under the shadow of Apollo's tree:
That plait their garlands fresh and well apaid,
And breathe forth lines of dainty poesy:
    Ah world, farewell, the sight hereof doth tell,
    That true content doth in the desert dwell.

See where a cave presents itself to eye,
By nature's hand enforced in marble veins;
Where climbing cedars with their shades deny
The eye of day to see what there remains:
    A couch of moss, a brook of silver clear,
    And more, for food, a flock of savage deer.

Then here (kind Muse) vouchsafe to dwell with me,
My velvet robe shall be a weed of gray,   50
And lest my heart by tongue betrayed be,
For idle talk I will go fast and pray:
    No sooner said and thought, but that my heart
    His true supposed content 'gan thus impart.

'Sweet solitary life, thou true repose,
Wherein the wise contemplate heaven aright:
In thee no dread of war or worldly foes,
In thee no pomp seduceth mortal sight,
    In thee no wanton ears to win with words,
    Nor lurking toys which city life affords.   60

At peep of day when in her crimson pride
The morn bespreads with roses all the way
Where Phoebus' coach with radiant course must glide,
The hermit bends his humble knees to pray:
    Blessing that God whose bounty did bestow
    Such beauties on the earthly things below.

Whether with solace tripping on the trees
He sees the citizens of Forest sport,
Or midst the withered oak beholds the bees
Intend their labour with a kind comfort: 70
    Down drops his tears, to think how they agree,
    Where men alone with hate inflamed be.

Taste he the fruits that spring from Tellus' womb;
Or drink he of the crystal spring that flows,
He thanks his God, and sighs their cursed doom
That fondly wealth in surfeiting bestows:
    And with Saint Jerome saith "The desert is
    A paradise of solace, joy and bliss."

Father of light, thou maker of the heaven,
From whom my being well, and being, springs:
Bring to effect this my desired steven,
That I may leave the thought of worldly things:
    Then in my troubles will I bless the time
    My Muse vouchsafed me such a lucky rhyme.'

15 · THOMAS LODGE

In every land from Gades to Ganges flood
Too few there be that think upon their good:
Too few that by discretion can discern
What profit rightly doth themselves concern.
Behold ambition's true-begotten son,
Spent in desire before his hope be won,
Striving for kingdoms which are sooner lost
Than kept, desired than had, with mighty cost;
Ending like him that senseless in his harms
Doth strive to stem a sea with two weak arms.
  Behold a mind pressing beyond his might,
Catching at stars, censured by oversight:
Like him that eager scales a mountain steep
And headlong falls into the valley deep.
There lives no man so settled in content
That hath not daily whereof to repent;
Nor can reformed wit so justly deem
But that it leaves true goods for such as seem.
Briefly, the greatest gifts whereof we boast
Are those which do attempt and tire us most.
Peace brings in pleasure, pleasure breeds excess,
Excess procureth want, want works distress,
Distress contempt; contempt is not repaired
Till timeless death determine hope despaired.
War eggs the victor to desire debate,
The conquered to submit and serve with hate;
Leaves nothing sure though he presume to choose,
But what he keeps with hate and dread to lose.

How oft hath watching policy devised
A cunning clause which hath himself surprised?   30
How often hath lewd fraud been set afloat
Of purpose that his goods might cut his throat?
Who builds on strength by policy is stripped:
Who trusts his wit, by wit is soonest tripped.
    Example be thou, Hepar, who, professed
A home-born infant of our English west,
Hast in that shameful scene of treason's play
Betrayed thyself to death, who wouldst betray:
Volcatius, that suborned, devised and wrought
To work out Themis from the place he sought,   40
Was laughed in court, and though he were not seen,
Yet wept his follies to a wooden screen.
Was never, since this wretched world began
To entertain, receive and nourish man,
A judgment by itself that never erred
Or wit unwronged by that he most preferred.
Travel the world, and traverse every clime,
And win one hour in every year of time;
Compass whate'er the sea receiveth round,
And seek to southward men of underground: 50
What hast thou got if following Candies' fate,
That keep'st no certain compass in thy state?
    O nought of ours, our wealth, our wit, enjoyed,
If not as ours, for us, it be employed:
Thy fame declining, Tellus, not thy farm,
Thy zeal, presumptuous Dacus, not thine arm;
Thy bounty, Varis, not thy many bribes,
Thy silence, Shanus, not thy many gibes.
These are those goods whereto you ought to cleave:
The rest are good in semblance, and deceive.   60
    What then in right for good may we elect?
Such things as challenge not by lewd respect.
Seek not in age with Crassus such a place
As both thy life and fortune may deface:
Nor fill the sea with sails, the earth with men,
In shameful sort, to be repulsed again;
Nor leave the northern lands, and fruitful Gaul,
In royal Rome thine empire to install.

For seldom can presumption be enthroned
To live esteemed, or die to be bemoaned.   70
    An humble cote entapissed with moss,
A lowly life that fears no sudden loss:
A mind that dreads no fall, nor craves no crown,
But makes his true content his best renown.
These are the choice contents, the goods, the gain
Which rightly can be ours: the rest are vain.
If thou then see a troop of guarded knaves
Wait at Argastos' heels like servile slaves,
Be not aghast, admire not at his state;
For now the world is bent to serve and hate.   80
'Tis true: that slave whom Pompey did promote
Was he that first assayed to cut his throat.

(A Fig for Momus, Satire V)

16 · JOHN DONNE

Well, I may now receive, and die: my sin
Indeed is great, but I have been in
A Purgatory such as feared hell is
A recreation to, and scant map of this.
My mind neither with pride's itch, nor yet hath been
Poisoned with love to see or to be seen;
I had no suit there, nor new suit to show,
Yet went to court. But as Glaze which did go
To a Mass in jest, catch'd, was fain to disburse
The hundred marks which is the statute's curse,   10
Before he 'scaped: so it pleased my destiny
(Guilty of my sin of going) to think me
As prone to all ill, and of good as forget-
ful, as proud, as lustful, and as much in debt,
As vain, as witless and as false as they
Which dwell at court, for once going that way.
    Therefore I suffered this: towards me did run
A thing more strange than on Nile's slime the sun
E'er bred, or all which into Noah's ark came—
A thing which would have posed Adam to name,   20

Stranger than seven antiquaries' studies,
Than Afric's monsters, Guiana's rarities;
Stranger than strangers; one who for a Dane
In the Danes' massacre had sure been slain
If he had lived then, and without help dies
When next the 'prentices 'gainst strangers rise.
One whom the watch at noon lets scarce go by;
One to whom the examining Justice sure would cry
'Sir, by your priesthood tell me what you are'.
His clothes were strange, though coarse, and black,
    though bare;   30
Sleeveless his jerkin was, and it had been
Velvet, but 'twas now (so much ground was seen)
Become tufftaffeta, and our children shall
See it plain rash awhile, then naught at all.
This thing hath travelled and (saith) speaks all tongues
And only knoweth what to all states belongs;
Made of the accents and best phrase of all these,
He speaks one language. If strange meats displease,
Art can deceive or hunger force my taste:
But pedants' motley tongue, soldiers' bombast,   40
Mountebanks' drug-tongue, nor the terms of law
Are strong enough preparatives to draw
Me to bear this: yet I must be content
With his tongue, in his tongue called compliment,
In which he can win widows and pay scores,
Make men speak treason, cozen subtlest whores,
Out-flatter favourites, or out-lie either
Jovius or Surius, or both together.
    He names me and comes to me; I whisper, 'God!
How have I sinned, that Thy wrath's furious rod,   50
This fellow, chooseth me?' He saith, 'Sir,
I love your judgment: whom do you prefer
For the best linguist?' And I sillily
Said that I thought Calepine's dictionary.
'Nay, but of men, most sweet sir?' Beza then,
Some Jesuits, and two reverend men
Of our two academies, I named. There
He stopped me and said 'Nay, your Apostles were
Good pretty linguists, and so Panurge was:

Yet a poor gentleman all these may pass   60
By travel.' Then, as if he would have sold
His tongue, he praised it, and such wonders told
That I was fain to say 'If you had lived, sir,
Time enough to have been interpreter
To Babel's bricklayers, sure the Tower had stood.'
He adds, 'If of court life you knew the good
You would leave loneness.' I said, 'Not alone
My loneness is. But Spartan's fashion,
To teach by painting drunkards, doth not taste
Now; Aretine's pictures have made few chaste;   70
No more can princes' courts, though there be few
Better pictures of vice, teach me virtue.'
He, like to a high-stretched lute-string, squeaked, 'O sir,
'Tis sweet to talk of kings'. 'At Wesminster',
Said I, 'the man that keeps the Abbey tombs,
And for his price doth with whoever comes
Of all our Harries and our Edwards talk,
From king to king and all their kin can walk:
Your ears shall hear naught but kings, your eyes meet
Kings only: the way to it is King-street.'   80
He smacked and cried 'He's base, mechanic, coarse;
So are all your Englishmen in their discourse.
Are not your Frenchmen neat?' 'Mine? As you see,
I have but one Frenchman—look, he follows me.'
'Certes they're neatly clothed; I of this mind am,
Your only wearing is your grogaram.'
'Not so, sir, I have more!' Under this pitch
He would not fly; I chaffed him. But, as itch
Scratched into smart, and as blunt iron ground
Into an edge, hurts worse, so I (fool) found   90
Crossing hurt me. To fit my sullenness
He to another key his style doth address
And asks 'What news?' I tell him of new plays.
He takes my hand: and, as a still which stays
A semibreve 'twixt each drop, he niggardly,
As loath to enrich me, so tells many a lie.
More than ten Holinsheds or Halls or Stows,
Of trivial household trash he knows. He knows
When the Queen frowned or smiled, and he knows what

A subtle statesman may gather of that;   100
He knows who loves whom, and who by poison
Hastes to an office's reversion;
He knows who hath sold his land, and now doth beg
A licence old iron, boots, shoes and egg-
shells to transport. Shortly boys shall not play
At span-counter or blow-point but they pay
Toll to some courtier. And, wiser than all us,
He knows what lady is not painted. Thus
He with home-meats tries me: I belch, spew, spit,
Look pale and sickly like a patient; yet   110
He thrusts me more. And, as if he undertook
To say Gallo-Belgicus without book
Speaks of all states and deeds that have been since
The Spaniards came, to the loss of Amiens;
Like a big wife at sight of loathed meat
Ready to travail: so I sigh and sweat
To hear this macaroon talk—in vain: for yet,
Either my humour or his own to fit,
He like a privileged spy, whom nothing can
Discredit, libels now 'gainst each great man.   120
He names a price for every office paid;
He saith our wars thrive ill because delayed;
That offices are entailed, and that there are
Perpetuities of them, lasting as far
As the last day, and that great officers
Do with the pirates share and Dunkirkers.
Who wastes in meat, in clothes, in horse, he notes:
Who loves whores, who boys, and who goats.
I—more amazed than Circe's prisoners when
They felt themselves turn beasts—felt myself then   130
Becoming traitor, and methought I saw
One of our giant statutes ope his jaw
To suck me in: for, hearing him, I found
That (as burnt venomed lechers do grow sound
By giving others their sores) I might grow
Guilty, and he free. Therefore I did show
All signs of loathing; but since I am in,
I must pay mine and my forefathers' sin
To the last farthing. Therefore to my power

Toughly and stubbornly I bear this cross. But the hour
Of mercy now was come. He tries to bring
Me to pay a fine to 'scape his torturing
And says 'Sir, can you spare me?' I said 'Willingly'.
'Nay sir, can you spare me a crown?' Thankfully I
Gave it as ransom: but as fiddlers still,
Though they be paid to be gone, yet needs will
Thrust one more jig upon you, so did he
With his long complimental thanks vex me.
But he is gone, thanks to his needy want
And the prerogative of my crown. Scant
His thanks were ended, when I (which did see
All the court filled with more strange things than he)
Ran from hence with such, or more, haste than one
Who fears more actions doth make from prison.
   At home in wholesome solitariness
My precious soul began the wretchedness
Of suitors at court to mourn, and a trance,
Like his who dreamt he saw hell, did advance
Itself on me: such men as he saw there
I saw at court, and worse, and more. Low fear
Becomes the guilty, not the accuser: then
Shall I, none's slave, of high-born or raised men
Fear frowns? and, my mistress Truth, betray thee
To the huffing, braggart, puffed nobility?
No, no: thou, which yesterday hast been
Almost about the whole world, hast thou seen,
O sun, in all thy journey, vanity
Such as swells the bladder of our court? I
Think he which made your waxen garden and
Transported it from Italy to stand
With us, at London, flouts our Presence: for
Just such gay painted things which no sap nor
Taste have in them, ours are; and natural
Some of their stocks are, their fruits bastard all.
   'Tis ten o'clock and past: all whom the mews,
Balloon, tennis, diet or the stews
Had all the morning held, now the second
Time made ready, that day, in flocks are found
In the Presence—and I (God pardon me!).

As fresh and sweet their apparels be, as be   180
The fields they sold to buy them. 'For a king
These hose are', cry the flatterers, and bring
Them next week to the Theatre to sell.
Wants reach all states: me seems they do as well
At stage, as court; all are players—whoe'er looks
(For themselves dare not go) o'er Cheapside books
Shall find their wardrobe's inventory. Now
The ladies come: as pirates, which do know
That there come weak ships fraught with cochineal,
The men board them, and praise, as they think, well   190
Their beauties, they the men's wits; both are bought.
Why good wits ne'er wear scarlet gowns I thought
This cause: these men men's wits for speeches buy
And women buy all reds which scarlets dye.
He called her beauty lime-twigs, her hair net;
She fears her drugs ill-laid, her hair loose-set.
Would not Heraclitus laugh to see Macrine
From hat to shoe himself at door refine
As if the Presence were a moschite, and lift
His skirts and hose, and call his clothes to shrift,   200
Making them confess not only mortal
Great stains and holes in them, but venial
Feathers and dust, wherewith they fornicate;
And then by Durer's rules survey the state
Of his each limb, and with strings the odds tries
Of his neck to his leg and waist to thighs.
So in immaculate clothes and symmetry
Perfect as circles—with such nicety
As a young preacher at his first time goes
To preach—he enters, and a lady which owes   210
Him not so much as good-will he arrests,
And unto her protests, protests, protests
So much as at Rome would serve to have thrown
Ten Cardinals into the Inquisition;
And whispered 'By Jesu' so often that a
Pursuivant would have ravished him away
For saying of Our Lady's psalter. But 'tis fit
That they each other plague: they merit it.
But here comes Glorius that will plague them both,

Who, in the other extreme, only doth
Call a rough carelessness good fashion;
Whose cloak his spurs tears, whom he spits on,
He cares not; his ill words do no harm
To him; he rusheth in, as if 'Arm, arm'
He meant to cry; and though his face be as ill
As theirs which in old hangings whip Christ, yet still
He strives to look worse; he keeps all in awe,
Jests like a licenced fool, commands like law.
    Tired, now I leave this place, and but pleased so
As men which from gaols to execution go,
Go through the great chamber (why is it hung
With the seven deadly sins?). Being among
Those Ascaparts—men big enough to throw
Charing Cross for a bar, men that do know
No token of worth but 'Queen's man' and fine
Living, barrels of beef, flagons of wine—
I shook like a spied spy. Preachers which are
Seas of wit and arts, you can, then dare
Drown the sins of this place, for, for me
Which am but a scarce brook, it enough shall be
To wash the stains away; though I yet
With Maccabees' modesty the known merit
    Of my work lessen, yet some wise man shall,
    I hope, esteem my writs canonical.

(Satire IV)

17 · JOHN DONNE

To Sir Henry Wotton

Sir, more than kisses letters mingle souls,
For thus friends absent speak. This ease controls
The tediousness of my life. But for these,
I could ideate nothing which could please,
But I should wither in one day, and pass
To a bottle of hay, that am a lock of grass.
    Life is a voyage, and in our life's ways
Countries, courts, towns, are rocks or remoras:

They break or stop all ships; yet our state's such
That (though than pitch they stain worse) we must touch.   10
If in the furnace of the even line
Or under the adverse icy Poles thou pine,
Thou know'st two temperate regions girded in
Dwell there. But oh, what refuge canst thou win,
Parched in the court and in the country frozen?
Shall cities, built of both extremes, be chosen?
Can dung and garlic be a perfume? or can
A scorpion and torpedo cure a man?
Cities are worst of all three: of all three
(O knotty riddle!) each is worst equally.   20
Cities are sepulchres, they who dwell there
Are carcases, as if no such there were;
And courts are theatres, where some men play
Princes, some slaves, all to one end and of one clay.
The country is a desert, where no good
Gained (as habits, not born) is understood.
There men become beasts and prone to more evils;
In cities blocks, and in a lewd court, devils.
As in the first chaos confusedly
Each element's qualities were in the other three;   30
So pride, lust, covetise, being several
To these three places, yet are all in all,
And mingled thus, their issue incestuous.
Falsehood is denizened; virtue is barbarous.
Let no man say there 'Virtue's flinty wall
Shall lock vice in me; I'll do none but know all.'
Men are sponges which, to pour out, receive;
Who know false play, rather than lose, deceive.
For in best understandings sin began:
Angels sinned first, then devils and then man.   40
Only perchance beasts sin not; wretched we
Are beasts in all but white integrity.
I think if men which in these places live
Durst look for themselves, and themselves retrieve,
They would like strangers greet themselves, seeing then
Utopian youth grown old Italian.
  Be then thine own home, and in thyself dwell:
In anywhere, continuance maketh hell.

And seeing the snail, which everywhere doth roam,
Carrying his own house still, still is at home, 50
Follow (for he is easy-paced) this snail,
Be thine own palace or the world's thy gaol.
And in the world's sea do not like cork sleep
Upon the water's face, nor in the deep
Sink like a lead without a line: but as
Fishes glide, leaving no print where they pass
Nor making sound, so closely thy course go:
Let men dispute whether thou breathe or no.
Only in this one thing be no Galenist: to make
Court's hot ambitions wholesome, do not take 60
A dram of country's dullness, do not add
Correctives, but (as chemics) purge the bad.
   But, sir, I advise not you; I rather do
Say o'er those lessons which I learned of you,
Whom (free from German schisms, and lightness
Of France, and fair Italy's faithlessness—
Having from these sucked all they had of worth
And brought home that faith which you carried forth)
I throughly love. But if myself I have won
To know my rules, I have and you have
Donne.

18 · JOSEPH HALL

I first adventure, with foolhardy might
To tread the steps of perilous despite;
I first adventure: follow me who list,
And be the second English satyrist.
Envy waits on my back, Truth on my side:
Envy will be my page and Truth my guide.
Envy the margent holds and Truth the line:
Truth doth approve but Envy doth repine.
For in this smoothing age who durst indite
Hath made his pen an hired parasite, 10

To claw the back of him that beastly lives
And prank base men in proud superlatives.
Whence damned vice is shrouded quite from shame
And crowned with virtue's meed, immortal name:
Infamy dispossessed of native due,
Ordained of old on looser life to sue:
The world's eye bleared with those shameless lies,
Masked in the show of meal-mouthed poesies.
Go, daring Muse, on with thy thankless task,
And do the ugly face of vice unmask: 20
And if thou canst not thy high flight remit
So as it might a lowly satyre fit,
Let lowly satyres rise aloft to thee:
Truth be thy speed and Truth thy patron be.

                              (*Virgidemiae*: *Prologue*)

19 · JOSEPH HALL

Great is the folly of a feeble brain,
O'erruled with love and tyrannous disdain:
For love, however in the basest breast
It breeds high thoughts that feed the fancy best,
Yet is he blind, and leads poor fools awry
While they hang gazing on their mistress' eye.
The love-sick poet, whose importune prayer
Repulsed is with resolute despair,
Hopeth to conquer his disdainful dame
With public plaints of his conceived flame.   10
Then pours he forth in patched sonnetings
His love, his lust and loathsome flatterings:
As though the staring world hanged on his sleeve,
When once he smiles, to laugh, and when he sighs, to
        grieve.
Careth the world, thou love, thou live, or die?
Careth the world how fair thy fair one be?
Fond wit-old, that wouldst load thy witless head
With timely horns, before thy bridal bed.

Then can he term his dirty ill-faced bride
Lady and queen and virgin deified: 20
Be she all sooty-black or berry-brown,
She's white as morrow's milk or flax new-blown.
And though she be some dunghill drudge at home
Yet can he her resign some refuse room
Amidst the well-known stars: or if not there,
Sure will he saint her in his Calendar.

(Virgidemiae, Book I Number VII)

20 · JOSEPH HALL

In the heavens' universal alphabet
All earthly things so surely are foreset,
That who can read those figures, may foreshow
Whatever thing shall afterwards ensue.
Fain would I know (might it our artist please)
Why can his tell-troth Ephemerides
Teach him the weather's state so long beforn,
And not foretell him nor his fatal horn,
Nor his death's-day, nor no such sad event
Which he might wisely labour to prevent?   10
    Thou damned mock-art, and thou brainsick tale
Of old astrology, where didst thou veil
Thy cursed head thus long, that so it missed
The black brands of some sharper satyrist?
Some doting gossip 'mongst the Chaldee wives
Did to the credulous world thee first derive:
And superstition nursed thee ever since
And published in profounder art's pretence:
That now, who pares his nails, or libs his swine,
But he must first take counsel of the sign.   20
So that the vulgar's count, for fair or foul,
For living or for dead, for sick or whole,
His fear or hope, for plenty or for lack,
Hangs all upon his New-year's Almanack.
If chance once in the spring his head should ache,
It was foretold: thus says mine almanack.

In the heavens' high-street are but a dozen rooms,
In which dwells all the world, past and to come:
Twelve goodly inns they are, with twelve fair signs,
Ever well-tended by our star-divines.   30
Every man's head inns at the horned Ram,
The whiles the neck the Black-bull's guest became:
Th' arms by good hap meet at the wrestling Twins,
The heart in the way at the Blue-lion inns.
The legs their lodging in Aquarius got,
That is Bridge-street of the heaven, I wot.
The feet took up the Fish with teeth of gold:
But who with Scorpio lodged may not be told.
    What office then doth the Star-gazer bear?
Or let him be the heavens' ostler,   40
Or tapsters some, or some be chamberlains,
To wait upon the guests they entertain.
Hence can they read, by virtue of their trade,
When anything is missed where it was laid.
Hence they divine, and hence they can devise,
If their aim fail, the stars to moralize.
Demon my friend, once liver-sick of love,
Thus learned I by the signs his grief remove.
In the blind Archer first I saw the sign,
When thou receiv'dst that wilful wound of thine: 50
And now in Virgo is that cruel maid
Which hath not yet with love thy love repaid.
But mark, when once it comes to Gemini,
Straightway Fish-whole shall thy sick liver be.
But now (as the angry heavens seem to threat)
Many hard fortunes and disasters great:
If chance it come to wanton Capricorn,
And so into the Ram's disgraceful horn,
Then learn thou of the ugly Scorpion
To hate her for her foul abusion: 60
Thy refuge then the Balance be of right,
Which shall thee from thy broken bond acquit:
So with the Crab go back whence thou began,
From thy first match: and live a single man.

                    (*Virgidemiae, Book II Number VII*)

                              105

When Gullion died (who knows not Gullion?)
And his dry soul arrived at Acheron,
He fair besought the ferryman of hell
That he might drink to dead Pantagruel.
Charon was 'fraid lest thirsty Gullion
Would have drunk dry the river Acheron,
Yet last consented for a little hire,
And down he dips his chops deep in the mire,
And drinks, and drinks, and swallows in the stream
Until the shallow shores all naked seem.   10
Yet still he drinks, nor can the boatman's cries,
Nor crabbed oars, nor prayers make him rise.
So long he drinks, till the black caravel
Stands still fast gravelled on the mud of hell.
There stand they still, nor can go nor retire,
Though greedy ghosts quick passage did require.
Yet stand they still, as though they lay at road,
Till Gullion his bladder would unload.
They stand and wait and pray for that good hour
Which when it came, they sailed to the shore.   20
But never since dareth the ferryman
Once entertain the ghost of Gullion.
Drink on, dry soul, and pledge sir Gullion:
Drink to all healths but drink not to thine own.

(Virgidemiae, Book III Number VI)

22 · JOSEPH HALL

Quid placet ergo?

I wot not how the world's degenerate,
That men or know or like not their estate:
Out from the Gades up to the eastern morn
Not one but holds his native state forlorn.
When comely stripling wish it were their chance
For Caenis' distaff to exchange their lance,

And wear curled periwigs, and chalk their face,
And still are poring on their pocket-glass.
Tired with pinned ruffs, and fans, and partlet-strips,
And busks, and farthingales about their hips;
And tread on corked stilts a prisoner's pace, 10
And make their napkin for their spitting-place,
And gripe their waist within a narrow span.
Fond Caenis that wouldst wish to be a man,
Whose mannish housewives like their refuse state
And make a drudge of their uxorious mate,
Who like a cot-quean freezeth at the rock,
While his breeched dame doth man the foreign stock.
    Is it not a shame to see each homely groom
Sit perched in an idle chariot-room, 20
That were not meet some pannel to bestride
Surcingled to a galled hackney's hide?
Each muck-worm will be rich with lawless gain,
Although he smother up mows of seven years' grain,
And hanged himself when corn grows cheap again;
Although he buy whole harvests in the spring
And foist in false strikes to the measuring:
Although his shop be muffled from the light
Like a day-dungeon, or Cimmerian night:
Nor full nor fasting can the carl take rest; 30
While his George-nobles rusten in his chest,
He sleeps but once and dreams of burglary,
And wakes, and casts about his frighted eye,
And gropes for thieves in every darker shade:
And if a mouse but stir, he calls for aid.
    The sturdy ploughman doth the soldier see
All scarfed with pied colours to the knee,
Whom Indian pillage hath made fortunate:
And now he 'gins to loathe his former state.
Now doth he inly scorn his Kendal-green, 40
And his patched cockers now despised been.
Nor list he now go whistling to the car,
But sells his team, and fettleth to the war.
O war, to them that never tried thee, sweet!
When his dead mate falls grovelling at his feet,
And angry bullets whistle at his ear,

And his dim eyes see nought but death and drear:
Oh happy ploughman, were thy weal well-known:
Oh happy all estates except his own!
Some drunken rhymer thinks his time well spent   50
If he can live to see his name in print:
Who when he is once fleshed to the press,
And sees his handsel have such fair success,
Sung to the wheel and sung unto the pail,
He sends forth thraves of ballads to the sale.
Nor then can rest, but volumes up bodged rhymes
To have his name talked of in future times.
The brain-sick youth that feeds his tickled ear
With sweet-sauced lies of some false traveller,
Which hath the Spanish Decades read awhile,   60
Or whetstone leasings of old Mandeville,
Now with discourses breaks his midnight sleep
Of his adventures through the Indian deep;
Of all their massy heaps of golden mines,
Or of the antique tombs of Palestine;
Or of Damascus' magic wall of glass,
Of Solomon his sweating piles of brass,
Of the bird Ruc that bears an elephant;
Of mermaids that the southern seas do haunt;
Of headless men; of savage cannibals;   70
The fashions of their lives and governals:
What monstrous cities there erected be,
Cairo, or the city of the Trinity.
Now are they dung-hill cocks, that have not seen
The bordering Alps or else the neighbour Rhine.
And now he plies the news-full Grasshopper,
Of voyages and ventures to enquire.
His land mortgaged, he sea-beat in the way
Wishes for home a thousand sithes a day:
And now he deems his home-bred fare as lief   80
As his parched brisket or his barrelled beef.
    'Mongst all these stirs of discontented strife
Oh let me lead an academic life,
To know much, and to think we nothing know;
Nothing to have, yet think we have enough,
In skill to want, and wanting seek for more,

In weal nor want, nor wish for greater store.
Envy ye monarchs, with your proud excess,
At our low sail and our high happiness.

(*Virgidemiae, Book IV Number VI*)

23 · JOSEPH HALL

PΩMH PYMH

Who says these Romish pageants been too high
To be the scorn of sportful poesy?
Certes, not all the world such matter wist
As are the seven hills for a satyrist.
Perdy, I loathe an hundred Matho's tongues,
An hundred gamesters' shifts, or landlords' wrongs,
Or Labeo's poems, or base Lolio's pride,
Or ever what I thought or wrote beside;
When once I think if carping Aquine's sprite
To see now Rome were licenced to the light,   10
How his enraged ghost would stamp and stare
That Caesar's throne is turned to Peter's chair.
To see an old shorn losel perched high
Crossing beneath a golden canopy,
The whiles a thousand hairless crowns crouch low
To kiss the precious case of his proud toe;
And for the lordly fasces borne of old,
To see two quiet crossed keys of gold,
Or Cybele's shrine, the famous Pantheon's frame,
Turned to the honour of Our Lady's name.   20
  But that he most would gaze and wonder at
Is the horned mitre and the bloody hat,
The crooked staff, their cowl's strange form and store—
Save that he saw the same in hell before;
To see their broken nuns with new-shorn heads
In a blind cloister toss their idle beads,
Or lousy cowls come smoking from the stews
To raise the lewd rent to their Lord accrues

(Who with rank Venice doth his pomp advance
By trading of ten thousand courtesans);   30
Yet backward must absolve a female's sin,
Like to a false dissembling Theatine,
Who when his skin is red with shirts of mail,
And rugged hair-cloth scours his greasy nail,
Or wedding-garment tames his stubborn back,
Which his hemp girdle dyes all blue and black;
Or of his alms-bowl three days supped and dined
Trudges to open stews of either kind;
Or takes some Cardinal's stable in the way,
And with some pampered mule doth wear the day,   40
Kept for his own lord's saddle when him list.
    Come, Valentine, and play the satyrist,
To see poor sucklings welcomed to the light
With searing-irons of some sour Jacobite,
Or golden offers of an aged fool
To make his coffin some Franciscan's cowl;
To see the Pope's black knight, a cloaked friar,
Sweating in the channel like a scavenger.
Whom erst thy bowed ham did lowly greet
When at the corner-cross thou didst him meet,   50
Tumbling his rosaries hanging at his belt,
Or his biretta, or his towered felt;
To see a lazy dumb acolythite
Armed against a devout fly's despite,
Which at the high altar doth the chalice vail
With a broad fly-flap of a peacock's tail,
The whiles the likerous priest spits every trice
With longing for his morning sacrifice,
Which he rears up quite perpendicular,
That the mid-church doth spite the chancel's fare,   60
Beating their empty maws that would be fed,
With the scant morsels of the sacrist's bread.
    Would he not laugh to death when he should hear
The shameless legends of Saint Christopher,
Saint George, the Sleepers, or Saint Peter's well,
Or of his daughter, good Saint Petronell?
But had he heard the female Father's groan,
Yeaning in midst of her procession;

Or now should see the needless trial-chair
(When each is proved by his bastard heir)   70
Or saw the churches, and new calendar
Pestered with mongrel saints, and relics dear;
Should he cry out on Codro's tedious tomes,
When his new rage would ask no narrower rooms?

(Virgidemiae, Book IV Number VII)

24 · JOHN MARSTON

A Cynic satyre

'A man, a man, a kingdom for a man!'
Why how now, currish mad Athenian,
Thou Cynic dog, seest not the streets do swarm
With troops of men? 'No, no, for Circe's charm
Hath turned them all to swine. I never shall
Think those same Samian saws authentical,
But rather, I dare swear, the souls of swine
Do live in men: for that same radiant shine,
That lustre wherewith Nature's nature decked
Our intellectual part—that gloss is soiled   10
With staining spots of vile impiety
And muddy dirt of sensuality.
These are no men, but apparitions,
Ignes fatui, glow-worms, fictions,
Meteors, rats of Nilus, fantasies,
Colosses, pictures, shades, resemblances.
                    Ho, Linceus!
Seest thou yon gallant in the sumptuous clothes?
How brisk, how spruce, how gorgeously he shows!
Note his French herring-bones, but note no more   20
Unless thou spy his fair appendant whore
That lackeys him. Mark nothing but his clothes,
His new-stamped complement, his cannon-oaths;
Mark those, for naught but such lewd viciousness
Ere graced him, save Sodom beastliness.

Is this a man? Nay, an incarnate devil
That struts in vice and glorieth in evil.'
    'A man, a man!' Peace, Cynic: yon is one.
A complete soul of all perfection.
'What? mean'st thou him that walks all open-breasted?   30
Drawn through the ear with ribands, plumy-crested?
He that doth snort in fat-fed luxury
And gapes for some grinding monopoly?
He that in effeminate invention,
In beastly source of all pollution,
In riot, lust and fleshly-seeming sweetness
Sleeps sound, secure, under the shade of greatness?
Mean'st thou that senseless, sensual epicure?
That sink of filth, that guzzle most impure?
What, he? Linceus, on my word thus presume,   40
He's nought but clothes and scenting sweet perfume.
His very soul, assure thee Linceus,
Is not so big as is an atomus:
Nay, he is spriteless, sense or soul hath none,
Since last Medusa turned him to a stone.'
    'A man, a man!' Lo, yonder I espy
The shade of Nestor in sad gravity;
Since old Silenus brake his ass's back
He now is forced his paunch and guts to pack
In a fair tumbril. Why, sour satyrist,   50
Canst thou unman him? Here I dare insist
And soothly say he is a perfect soul,
Eats nectar, drinks ambrosia sans control.
An inundation of felicity
Fats him with honour and huge treasury.
'Canst thou not, Linceus, cast thy searching eye
And spy his imminent catastrophe?
He's but a sponge, and shortly needs must leese
His wrong-got juice, when greatness' fist shall squeeze
His liquor out. Would not some shallow head   60
That is with seeming shadows only fed
Swear yon same damask-coat, yon guarded man,
Were some grave sober Cato Utican?
When let him but in judgment's sight uncase,
He's naught but budge, old guards, brown fox-fur face.

He hath no soul, the which the Stagirite
Termed rational; for beastly appetite,
Base dunghill thoughts, and sensual action
Hath made him lose that fair creation.
And now no man, since Circe's magic charm   70
Hath turned him to a maggot, that doth swarm
In tainted flesh, whose foul corruption
Is his fair food, whose generation
Another's ruin. O Canaan's dread curse,
To live in people's sins! Nay, far more worse
To muck rank hate. But sirrah, Linceus,
See'st thou that troop that now affronteth us?
They are naught but eels, that never will appear
Till that tempestuous winds or thunder tear
Their slimy beds. But prithee, stay awhile: 80
Look, yon comes John-a-noake and John-a-style:
They're naught but slow-paced dilatory pleas,
Demure demurrers, still striving to appease
Hot zealous love: the language that they speak
Is the pure barbarous blacksaunt of the Geat;
Their only skill rests in collusions,
Abatements, stoppels, inhibitions;
Heavy-paced jades, dull-pated jobbernolls,
Quick in delays, checking with vain controls
Fair justice' course, vile necessary evils,   90
Smooth seem-saints, yet damned incarnate devils.
    Far be it from my sharp satyric muse
Those grave and reverend legists to abuse
That aid Astraea, that do further right:
But these Megaeras that inflame despite,
That broach deep rancour, that do study still
To ruin right, that they their paunch may fill
With Irus' blood, these Furies I do mean,
These hedgehogs that disturb Astraea's scene.
    A man, a man!' Peace, Cynic, yon's a man: 100
Behold yon spritely dread Mavortian:
With him I stop thy currish barking chops.
'What? mean'st thou him, that in his swaggering slops
Wallows unbraced all along the street?
He that salutes each gallant he doth meet

113

With "Farewell, sweet captain, kind heart, adieu".
He that last night tumbling thou didst view
From out the Great Man's Head, and thinking still
He had been sentinel of warlike Brill,
Cries out "Qui va la?"—zounds, qui! and out doth draw   110
His transformed poignard to a syringe-straw
And stabs the drawer. What, that 'ringo-root?
Mean'st thou that wasted leg, puff-bombast boot?
What? he that's drawn and quartered with lace?
That Westphalian-gammon clove-stuck face?
Why, he is naught but huge blaspheming oaths,
Swart-snout, big-looks, misshapen Switzer's clothes.
Weak meagre lust hath now consumed quite
And wasted clean away his martial sprite;
Enfeebling riot, all vices' confluence,   120
Hath eaten out that sacred influence
Which made him man.
That divine part is soaked away in sin,
In sensual lust and midnight bezzling.
Rank inundation of luxuriousness
Have tainted him with such gross beastliness
That now the seat of that celestial essence
Is all possessed with Naples pestilence.
Fat peace and dissolute impiety
Have lulled him in such security,   130
That now let whirlwinds and confusions tear
The centre of our state, let giants rear
Hill upon hill, let western Termagant
Shake heaven's vault,—he with his occupant
Are clinged so close, like dew-worms in the morn,
That he'll not stir till out his guts are torn
With eating filth. Tubrio, snort on, snort on
Till thou art waked with sad confusion.
    Now rail no more at my sharp Cynic sound,
Thou brutish world, that in all vileness drowned   140
Hast lost thy soul, for naught but shades, I see,
Resemblances of men, inhabit thee.
    Yon tissue-slop, yon holy-crossed pane
Is but a water-spaniel that will fawn
And kiss the water whilst it pleasures him,

114

But being once arrived at the brim
He shakes it off.
    Yon in the capering cloak, a mimic ape,
That only strives to seem another's shape,
Yon's Aesop's ass; yon sad civility 150
Is but an ox that with base drudgery
Ears up the land, whilst some gilt ass doth chaw
The golden wheat; he well apaid with straw.
Yon's but a muck-hill overspread with snow
Which with that veil doth even as fairly show
As the green meads, whose native outward fair
Breathes sweet perfumes into the neighbour air.
Yon effeminate sanguine Ganymede
Is but a beaver, hunted for the bed.'
    Peace, Cynic, see what yonder doth approach. 160
'A cart, a tumbril?' No, a badged coach.
'What's in 't? some man?' No, nor yet woman kind,
But a celestial angel, fair refined.
'The devil as soon. Her mask so hinders me,
I cannot see her beauty's deity.
Now that is off, she is so vizarded,
So steeped in lemons' juice, so surphuled
I cannot see her face. Under one hood
Two faces, but I never understood
Or saw one face under two hoods till now: 170
'Tis the right semblance of old Janus' brow.
    Her mask, her vizard, her loose-hanging gown
For her loose-lying body, her bright spangled crown,
Her long-slit sleeve, stiff busk, puff farthingale,
Is all that makes her thus angelical.
Alas, her soul struts round about her neck,
Her seat of sense is her rebato set,
Her intellectual is a feigned niceness:
Nothing but clothes and simpering preciseness.
    Out on these puppets, painted images, 180
Haberdashers' shops, torch-light maskeries,
Perfuming-pans, Dutch ancients, glow-worms bright
That soil our souls and damp our reason's light:
Away, away, hence coachman, go enshrine
Thy new-glazed puppet in Port Esquiline.

Blush, Martia, fear not or look pale: all's one:
Margara keeps thy set complexion.
　Sure, I ne'er think those axioms to be true,
That souls of men from that great soul ensue,
And of his essence do participate   190
As 't were by pipes: when so degenerate,
So adverse is our nature's motion
To his immaculate condition:
That such foul filth from such fair purity,
Such sensual acts from such a Deity
Can ne'er proceed. But if that dream were so,
Then sure the slime that from our souls do flow
Have stopped those pipes by which it was conveyed,
And now no human creatures, once disrayed
Of that fair gem.   200
Beasts' *sense*, plants' *growth*, like *being* as a stone:
But out, alas, our *cognisance* is gone.'

(The Scourge of Villainy, Satire VII)

25 · JOHN MARSTON

In serious jest and jesting seriousness
I strive to scourge polluting beastliness.
I invoke no Delian deity,
Nor sacred offspring of Mnemosyne;
I pray in aid of no Castalian muse,
No nymph, no female angel to infuse
A spritely wit to raise my flagging wings
And teach me tune these harsh discordant strings.
I crave no Sirens of our halcyon times
To grace the accents of my rough-hewed rhymes,   10
But grim reproof, stern hate of villainy,
Inspire and guide a satyre's poesy.
Fair detestation of foul odious sin
In which our swinish times lie wallowing,
Be thou my conduct and my genius,
My wits-inciting sweet-breath'd Zephyrus.

O that a satyre's hand had force to pluck
Some floodgate up, to purge the world from muck:
Would God I could turn Alpheus' river in
To purge this Augean ox-stall from foul sin.   20
    Well, I will try: awake impurity,
    And view the veil drawn from thy villainy.

(*The Scourge of Villainy, Proemium to Book III*)

26 · JOHN MARSTON

Inamorato Curio

Curio, aye me, thy mistress' monkey's dead!
Alas, alas, her pleasure's buried.
Go, woman's slave, perform his exequies;
Condole his death in mournful elegies.
Tut, rather paeans sing, hermaphrodite,
For that sad death gives life to thy delight.
    Sweet-faced Corinna, deign the riband tie
Of thy cork-shoe, or else thy slave will die;
Some puling sonnet tolls his passing-bell,
Some sighing elegy must ring his knell: 10
Unless bright sunshine of thy grace revive
His wambling stomach, certes he will dive
Into the whirlpool of devouring death
And to some mermaid sacrifice his breath.
Then oh, oh then, to thy eternal shame,
And to the honour of sweet Curio's name,
This epitaph upon the marble stone
Must fair be graved of that true loving one:
            Here lieth he, he lieth here
                that bounced, and pity cried;   20
            The door not oped, fell sick alas,
                alas fell sick and died.
What Myrmidon or hard Dolopian,
What savage-minded rude Cyclopian,
But such a sweet pathetic Paphian

117

Would force to laughter? Ho, Amphitryon,
Thou art no cuckold: what though Jove dallied,
During thy wars, in fair Alcmena's bed?
Yet Hercules true-born, that imbecility
Of corrupt nature all apparently   30
Appears in him, o foul indignity!
I heard him vow himself a slave to Omphale,
Puling (aye me) o valour's obloquy!
He that the inmost nooks of hell did know,
Whose ne'er-crazed prowess all did overthrow,
Lies streaking brawny limbs in weakening bed,
Perfumed, smooth-kempt, new-glazed, fair-surphuled.
O that the boundless power of the soul
Should be subjected to such base control!
    Big-limbed Alcides, doff thy honour's crown;   40
Go spin, huge slave, lest Omphale should frown.
By my best hopes, I blush with grief and shame
To broach the peasant baseness of our name.
    O now my ruder hand begins to quake,
To think what lofty cedars I must shake:
But if the canker fret the barks of oaks,
Like humbler shrubs shall equal bear the strokes
Of my respectless rude satyric hand.
    Unless the Destin's adamantine hand
Should tie my teeth, I cannot choose but bite,   50
To view Mavortius metamorphosed quite
To puling sighs and into 'aye me's' state,
With voice distinct, all fine articulate
Lisping 'Fair saint, my woe compassionate;
By heaven, thine eye is my soul-guiding fate.'
    The god of wounds had wont on Cyprian couch
To streak himself, and with incensing touch
To faint his force only when wrath had end:
But now, 'mong furious garboils, he doth spend
His feebled valour in tilt and tourneying,   60
With wet-turned kisses melting, dallying.
A pox upon't, that Bacchis' name should be
The watchword given to the soldiery.
Go, troop to field, mount thy obscured fame,
Cry out St George, invoke thy mistress's name;

Thy mistress, and St George, alarum cry!
Weak force, weak aid, that sprouts from luxury.
　　Thou tedious workmanship of lust-stung Jove,
Down from thy skies, enjoy our females' love;
Some fifty more Boeotian girls will sue   70
To have thy love, so that thy back be true.
　　O now methinks I hear swart Martius cry,
Sweeping along in war's fained maskery,
By Lais' starry front he'll forthwith die
In cluttered blood, his mistress' livery.
Her fancy's colours waves upon his head.
O well-fenced Albion, mainly manly sped,
When those that are soldados in thy state
Do bear the badge of base, effeminate,
Even on their plumy crests, brutes sensual,   80
Having no spark of intellectual.
Alack, what hope? when some rank nasty wench
Is subject of their vows and confidence?
　　Publius hates vainly to idolatries
And laughs that Papists honour images:
And yet (o madness) these mine eyes did see
Him melt in moving plaints, obsequiously
Imploring favour, twining his kind arms,
Using enchantments, exorcisms, charms,
The oil of sonnets, wanton blandishment,   90
The force of tears and seeming languishment,
Unto the picture of a painted lass.
I saw him court his mistress' looking-glass,
Worship a busk-point (which in secrecy
I fear was conscious of strange villainy).
I saw him crouch, devote his livelihood,
Swear, protest, vow peasant servitude
Unto a painted puppet; to her eyes
I heard him swear his sighs to sacrifice.
But if he get her itch-allaying pin—   100
O sacred relic—straight he must begin
To rave outright, then thus: 'Celestial bliss,
Can heaven grant so rich a grace as this?
Touch it not, by the Lord, sir, 'tis divine:
It once beheld her radiant eyes' bright shine;

Her hair embraced it: o thrice-happy prick
That there was throned, and in her hair didst stick.'
Kiss, bless, adore it, Publius, never lin:
Some sacred virtue lurketh in the pin.
   O frantic fond pathetic passion! 110
Is't possible such sensual action
Should clip the wings of contemplation?
O can it be the spirit's function,
The soul, not subject to dimension,
Should be made slave to reprehension
Of crafty Nature's paint? Fie, can our soul
Be underling to such a vile control?
   Saturio wished himself his mistress' busk
That he might sweetly lie and softly lusk
Between her paps; then must he have an eye 120
At either end, that freely might descry
Both hills and dales. But out on Phrigio,
That wished he were his mistress' dog, to go
And lick her milk-white fist. O pretty grace,
That pretty Phrigio begs but Pretty's place!
Parthenophil, thy wish I will omit:
So beastly 'tis I may not utter it.
But Punicus, of all I'll bear with thee,
That fain wouldst be thy mistress' smug monkey.
Here's one would be a flea (jest comical), 130
Another his sweet lady's farthingale
To clip her tender breech. Another he
Her silver-handled fan would gladly be.
Here's one would be his mistress' necklace fain,
To clip her fair, and kiss her azure vein.
Fond fools, well-wished, and pity but should be,
For beastly shape to brutish souls agree.
   If Laura's painted lip do deign a kiss
To her enamoured slave, 'O heaven's bliss'
(Straight he exclaims) 'not to be matched with this!' 140
Blaspheming dolt, go three score sonnets write
Upon a picture's kiss, o raving sprite!
   I am not sapless, old or rheumatic,
No Hipponax, misshapen, stigmatic,
That I should thus inveigh 'gainst amorous sprite

Of him whose soul doth turn hermaphrodite;
But I do sadly grieve, and inly vex,
To view the base dishonours of our sex.
 Tush, guiltless doves, when gods to force foul rapes
Will turn themselves to any brutish shapes.   150
Base bastard powers, whom the world doth see
Transformed to swine for sensual luxury.
The son of Saturn is become a bull
To crop the beauties of some female trull.
Now, when he hath his first wife Metim sped
And fairly choked, lest fool-gods should be bred
Of that fond mule, Themis his second wife
Hath turned away, that his unbridled life
Might have more scope. Yet last his sister's love
Must satiate the lustful thoughts of Jove.   160
Now doth the lecher in a cuckoo's shape
Commit a monstrous and incestuous rape.
Thrice sacred gods, and o thrice blessed skies,
Whose orbs includes such virtuous deities!
 What should I say? Lust hath confounded all;
The bright gloss of our intellectual
Is foully soiled. The wanton wallowing
In fond delights and amorous dallying
Hath dusked the fairest splendour of our soul:
Nothing now left but carcass, loathsome, foul.   170
For sure, if that some sprite remained still,
Could it be subject to lewd Lais' will?
 Reason by prudence in her function
Had wont to tutor all our action,
Aiding with precepts of philosophy
Our feebled nature's imbecility.
But now affection, will, concupiscence,
Have got o'er reason chief pre-eminence.
'Tis so; else how, how should such baseness taint
As force it be made slave to Nature's paint?   180
Methinks the spirit's Pegase-fantasy
Should hoise the soul from such base slavery.
But now I see, and can right plainly show,
From whence such abject thoughts and actions grow.
 Our adverse body, being earthly, cold,

Heavy, dull, mortal, would not long enfold
A stranger inmate that was backward still
To all his dungy, brutish, sensual will.
Now hereupon, our intellectual,
Compact of fire all celestial,   190
Invisible, immortal and divine,
Grew straight to scorn his landlord's muddy slime;
And therefore now is closely slunk away
(Leaving his smoky house of mortal clay)
Adorned with all his beauty's lineaments
And brightest gems of shining ornaments,
His parts divine, sacred, spiritual,
Attending on him, leaving the sensual
Base hangers-on lusking at home in slime,
Such as wont to stop Port Esquiline.   200
Now doth the body led with senseless will
(The which in reason's absence ruleth still)
Rave, talk idly, as 't were some deity
Adoring female painted puppetry
Playing at put-pin, doting on some glass
(Which, breathed but on, his falsed gloss doth pass),
Toying with babies, and with fond pastime,
Some children's sport, deflowering of chaste time,
Employing all his wits in vain expense,
Abusing all his organons of sense.   210
     Return, return, sacred synderesis,
Inspire our trunks; let not such mud as this
Pollute us still. Awake our lethargy,
Raise us from out our brain-sick foolery.

                             (*The Scourge of Villainy, Satire VIII*)

27 · EVERARD GUILPIN

Let me alone, I prithee, in this cell:
Entice me not into the city's hell;
Tempt me not forth this Eden of content
To taste of that which I shall soon repent.

Prithee excuse me, I am not alone—
Accompanied with meditation
And calm content, whose taste more pleaseth me
Than all the city's luscious vanity.
I had rather be encoffined in this chest
Amongst these books and papers (I protest)   10
Than free-booting abroad purchase offence
And scandal my calm thoughts with discontents.
Here I converse with those diviner spirits
Whose knowledge and admire the world inherits:
Here doth the famous profound Stagirite
With Nature's mystic harmony delight
My ravished contemplation: I here see
The now old world's youth in an history.
Here may I be grave Plato's auditor,
And learning of that moral lecturer   20
To temper mine affections, gallantly
Get of myself a glorious victory.
And then for change, as we delight in change
(For this my study is indeed my Exchange),
Here may I sit, yet walk to Westminster
And hear Fitzherbert, Plowden, Brooke and Dyer
Canvass a law-case: or if my dispose
Persuade me to a play, I'll to the Rose
Or Curtain—one of Plautus' comedies
Or the pathetic Spaniard's tragedies.   30
If my desire doth rather wish the fields,
Some speaking painter, some poet straightway yields
A flower-bespangled walk, where I may hear
Some amorous swain his passions declare
To his sun-burnt love. Thus my books' little case,
My study, is mine All, mine every place.
   What more variety of pleasures can
An idle city-walk afford a man?
More troublesome and tedious, well I know
'Twill be, into the peopled streets to go: 40
Witness that hotch-potch of so many noises,
Blacksaunts of so many several voices,
That chaos of rude sounds, that harmony
And diapason of harsh barbary

123

Composed of several mouths and several cries
Which to men's ears turn both their tongues and eyes.
There squeaks a cart-wheel, here a tumbril rumbles,
Here scolds an old bawd, there a porter grumbles.
Here two tough car-men combat for the way;
There two for looks begin a coward fray; 50
Two swaggering knaves here brabble for a whore,
There brawls an ale-knight for his fat-grown score.
   But oh purgation! yon rotten-throated slaves
Engarlanded with cony-catching knaves,
Whores, beadles, bawds and sergeants filthily
Chant Kemp's jig or the Burgonian's tragedy:
But in good time, there's one hath nipped a bong—
Farewell, my hearts, for he hath marred the song.
   Yet might all this, this too bad be excused,
Were not an ethic soul much more abused 60
And her still patience choked by vanity
With unsufferable inhumanity.
For whose gall is't that would not overflow
To meet, in every street where he shall go,
With folly masked in divers semblances?
The city is the map of vanities,
The mart of fools, the magazine of gulls,
The painter's shop of antics: walk in Paul's,
And but observe the sundry kinds of shapes,
Thou wilt swear that London is as rich in apes 70
As Afric Tabraca. One wries his face:
This fellow's wry-neck is his better grace.
He coined in newer mint of fashion,
With the right Spanish shrug shows passion;
There comes one in a muffler of Cadiz-beard
Frowning as he would make the world afeared;
With him a troop all in gold-daubed suits,
Looking like Talbots, Percys, Montacutes,
As if their very countenances would swear
The Spaniards should conclude a peace for fear. 80
But bring them to a charge, then see the luck:
Though but a false fire they their plumes will duck.
What marvel, since life's sweet? But see yonder,
One like the unfrequented theatre

Walks in dark silence and vast solitude
Suited to those black fancies which intrude
Upon possession of his troubled breast:
But for black's sake he would look like a jest
For he's clean out of fashion. 'What, he?'
'I think the genius of antiquity   90
Come to complain of our variety
Of tickle fashions.' 'Then you jest, I see.'
'Would you needs know? He is a malcontent.'
'A Papist?' 'No, nor yet a Protestant,
But a discarded intelligencer.'
Here's one looks like to a King Arthur's fencer,
With his case of rapiers, and suited in buff:
Is he not a sergeant? Then say 's a muff
For his furred satin cloak: but let him go,
Meddle not with him, he's a shrewd fellow!   100
   Oh what a pageant's this? what fool was I
To leave my study to see vanity?
But who's in yonder coach? my lord and fool,
One that for ape-tricks can put Gue to school:
Heroic spirits, true nobility
Which can make choice of such society!
He more perfections hath than y' would suppose:
He hath a wit of wax, fresh as a rose;
He plays well on the treble violin;
He soothes his lord up in his grossest sin.   110
At any rhymes sprung from his lordship's head,
Such as Elderton would not have fathered,
He cries 'Oh rare, my lord!' He can discourse
The story of Don Pacolet and his horse
(To make my lord laugh), swear and jest
And with a simile nonplus the best
(Unless like Pace his wit be over-awed):
But his best part is, he's a perfect bawd.
Rare virtues, farewell they! But who's yonder
Deep-mouthed hound that bellows rhymes like thunder?   120
He makes an earthquake throughout Paul's churchyard!
Well fare his heart, his 'larum shall be heard.
Oh, he's a puisne of the Inns of court
Come from the University to make sport

With his friends' money here, But see, see,
Here comes Don Fashion, spruce formality,
Neat as a merchant's ruff that's set in print,
New halfpenny, skipped forth his laundress' mint;
Oh brave! what, with a feather in his hat?
He is a dancer, you may see by that:
Light heels, light head, light feathers well agree.
Salute him, with th' embrace beneath the knee?
I think 'twere better let him pass along—
He will so daub us with his oily tongue:
For thinking on some of his mistresses
We shall be curried with the brisk phrases
And prick-song terms he hath premeditate.
Speak to him? woe to us, for we shall have 't.
Then farewell he! But soft, whom have we here?
What brave Saint George, what mounted cavalier?
He is all court-like, Spanish in 's attire:
He hath the right duck, pray God he be no friar.
This is the dictionary of compliments,
The barber's mouth of new-scraped eloquence,
Synomic Tully for variety,
And Madame Conceit's gorgeous gallery—
The exact pattern which Castilio
Took for 's accomplished courtier! But soft ho,
What needs that bound or that curvet, good sir?
There's some sweet lady, and 'tis done to her
That she may see his jennet's nimble force:
Why, would he have her in love with his horse?
Or aims he at popish merit, to make
Her in love with him for his horse's sake?
     The further that we walk, more vanity
Presents itself to prospect of mine eye.
Here swears some seller—though a known untruth—
Here's his wife bated by some quick-chapped youth.
There in that window Mistress Minx doth stand
And to some copemate beckoneth her hand:
In is he gone, Saint Venus be his speed,
For some great thing must be adventured.
There comes a troop of puisnes from the play
Laughing like wanton schoolboys all the way.

130

140

150

160

Yon go a knot to Bloom's ordinary—
Friends and good fellows all now, by and by
They'll be by the ears, vie stabs, exchange disgraces,
And bandy daggers at each other's faces.
    Enough of these, then, and enough of all:
I may thank you for this time spent, but call   170
Henceforth I'll keep my study, and eschew
The scandal of my thoughts, my folly's view:
Now let us home, I'm sure 'tis supper-time,
The horn hath blown, have done my merry rhyme.

(Skialetheia, Satire V)

28 · [T.M.]

Cheating Droone

There is a cheater by profession
That takes more shapes than the chameleon.
Sometimes he jets it in a black-furred gown—
And that is when he harbours in the town;
Sometimes a cloak to mantle hoary age,
Ill-favoured like an ape in spiteful rage:
And then he walks in Paul's a turn or two
To see by cheating what his wit can do.
    Perhaps he'll tell a gentleman a tale
Will cost him twenty angels in the sale: 10
But if he know his purse well-lined within,
And by that means he cannot finger him,
He'll proffer him such far-fetched courtesy
That shortly in a tavern neighbouring by
He hath encaged the silly gentleman,
To whom he proffers service all he can.
    'Sir, I perceive you are of gentle blood,
Therefore I will our cates be new and good:
For well I wot, the country yieldeth plenty,
And as they diverse be, so are they dainty.   20
May it please you then awhile to rest you merry;
Some cates I will make choice of and not tarry.'

The silly cony blithe and merrily
Doth for his kindness thank him heartily.
Then hies the cheater very hastily
And with some peasant where he is in fee
Juggles that (dinner being almost ended)
He in a matter of weight may then be friended.
The peasant for an angel then in hand
Will do whate'er his worship shall command, 30
And yields that, when a reckoning they call in,
To make reply there's one to speak with him.
 The plot is laid; now comes the cheater back
And calls in haste for such things as they lack:
The table freighted with all dainty cates,
Having well-fed, they fall to pleasant chats:
Discoursing of the mickle difference
'Twixt perfect truth and painted eloquence:
Plain truth, that harbours in the country swain,
The cony stands defendant; the cheater's vein 40
Is to uphold an eloquent smooth tongue,
To be truth's orator righting every wrong.
 Before the cause concluded took effect,
In comes a crew of fiddling knaves abject,
The very refuse of that rabble rout,
Half-shoes upon their feet torn round about—
Save little Dick the dapper singing knave:
He had a threadbare coat to make him brave,
God knows, scarce worth a tester, if it were
Valued, at most, of seven, it were too dear! 50
Well, take it as they list, shake-rag came in,
Making no doubt but that they would like of him:
And, 'twere but for his person, a pretty lad,
Well qualified, having a singing trade.
Well, so it was; the cheater must be merry,
And he a song must have called Hey Down Derry.
So Dick begins to sing, the fiddler play;
The melancholy cony replies 'Nay, nay,
No more of this.' The 'tother bids play on—
' 'Tis good our spirits should something work upon. 60
Tut, gentle sir, be pleasant, man' (quoth he);
'Yours be the pleasure, mine the charge shall be.

This do I for the love of gentlemen;
Hereafter happily if we meet again
I shall of you expect like courtesy,
Finding fit time and opportunity.'
  'Or else I were ungrateful', quoth the cony.
'It shall go hard but we will find some money.
For some we have; that some well-used gets more;
And so in time we shall increase our store.   70
Meantime', said he, 'employ it to good use;
For time ill-spent doth purchase time's abuse.'
  With that, more wine he calls for, and intends
That either of them carouse all their friends.
The cony nods the head, yet says not nay,
Because the other would the charge defray.
  The end tries all; and here begins the jest:
My gentleman betook him to his rest.
Wine took possession of his drowsy head,
And cheating Droone hath brought the fool to bed.   80
The fiddlers were discharged, and all things whist;
Then pilfering Droone 'gan use him as he list.
Ten pound he finds, the reckoning he doth pay,
And with the residue passeth sheer away.
Anon the cony wakes; his coin being gone
He exclaims against dissimulation.
But 'twas too late; the cheater had his prey.
Be wise, young heads, care for an after-day!

(Micro-Cynicon, Satire IV)

29 · SAMUEL ROWLANDS

Who have we here? Behold him and be mute!
Some mighty man, I'll warrant, by his suit:
If all the mercers in Cheapside show such,
I'll give them leave to give me twice as much.
I think the stuff is nameless he doth wear,
But whatsoe'er it be, it is huge gear.

Mark but his gait, and give him but his due,
Some swaggering fellow, I may say to you.
It seems ambition in his big looks shrouds
Some Centaur, sure, begotten of the clouds.   10
Now a shame take the buzzard, is it he?
I know the ruffian now his face I see.
On a more gull the sun did never shine:
How with a vengeance comes the fool so fine?
Some nobleman's cast suit is fallen unto him,
For buying hose and doublet would undo him.
    But wot you now whither the buzzard walks?
Aye, into Paul's forsooth: and there he talks
Of foreign tumults, uttering his advice
And proving war's even like a game at dice: 20
For this (says he) as every gamester knows,
Where one side wins, the other side must lose.
Next speech he utters is his stomach's care,
Which ordinary yields the cheapest fare—
Or if his purse be out of tune to pay,
Then he remembers 'tis a fasting-day;
And then he talketh much against excess,
Swearing all other nations eat far less
Than Englishmen: experience you may get
In France and Spain—where he was never yet.   30
'With a score of figs and half a pint of wine
Some four or five will very hugely dine.'
Methinks this tale is very huge in sound,
That half a pint should serve five to drink round,
And twenty figs could feed them full and fat—
But travellers may lie: who knows not that?
Then why not he who travels in conceit
From east to west, when he can get no meat?
His journey is in Paul's in the back aisles,
Where 's stomach counts each pace a hundred miles.   40
A tedious thing, though chance will have it such,
To travel so long baitless, sure 'tis much.
    Some other time, stumbling on wealthy chuffs
Worth gulling, then he swaggers all in huffs,
And tells them of a prize he was at taking,
Will be the ship-boy's children's children's making;

And that a mouse could find no room in hold,
It was so pestered all with pearl and gold:
Vowing to pawn his head if it were tried
They had more rubies than would pave Cheapside.   50
A thousand other gross and odious lies
He dares avouch to blind dull judgment's eyes,
Not caring what he speak or what he swear,
So he gain credit at his hearer's ear.
   Sometimes into the Royal Exchange he'll drop,
Clad in the ruins of a broker's shop:
And there his tongue runs bias on affairs,
No talk but of commodities and wares,
And what great wealth he looks for every wind
From God knows where—the place is hard to find.   60
If news be hearkened for, then he prevails,
Setting his mint a-work to coin false tales.
His tongue's end is betipped with forged chat,
Uttering lies to be admired at.
He'll tell you of a tree that he doth know
Upon the which rapiers and daggers grow
As good as Fleet-street hath in any shop,
Which being ripe, down into scabbards drop.
He hath a very piece of that same chair
In which Caesar was stabbed: is it not rare?   70
He with his feet upon the stones did tread
That Satan brought, and bade Christ make the bread.
His wondrous travels challenge such renown
That Sir John Mandeville is quite put down:
Men without heads, and pygmies hand-breadth high,
Those with one leg that on their backs do lie
And do the weather's injury disdain,
Making their legs a penthouse for the rain,
Are tut and tush, not anything at all.
His knowledge knows what no man notice shall.   80
This is a mate unmeet for every groom,
And where he comes, peace, give him lying-room.
He saw a Hollander in Middelburg,
As he was slashing of a brown loaf thorough
(Whereto the haste of hunger had inclined him)
Cut himself through, and two that stood behind him.

Besides, he saw a fellow put to death
Could drink a whole beer-barrel at a breath.
Oh, this is he that will say anything
That to himself may any profit bring.   90
'Gainst whosoever he doth speak he cares not,
For what is it that such a villain dares not?
And though in conscience he cannot deny
The All-Commander saith 'Thou shalt not lie',
Yet will he answer (careless of soul's state):
'Truth-telling is a thing obtaineth hate.'

(*The Letting of Humour's Blood in the Head-Vein, Satire I*)

30 · SAMUEL ROWLANDS

Oh let the gentlewoman have the wall:
I know her well, 'tis Mistress What d'ye call.
It should be she, both by her mask and fan:
And yet it should not, by her serving-man.
For if mine eyes do not mistake the fool,
He is the usher of some dancing-school.
The reason why I do him such suppose
Is this: methinks he danceth as he goes.
An active fellow, though he be but poor,
Either to vault upon a horse or &c.   10
See you the huge bum-dagger at his back
To which no hilt or iron he doth lack?
Oh with that blade he keeps the queans in awe,
Bravely behacked, like a two-hand saw;
Stamps on the ground and biteth both his thumbs
Unless he be commander where he comes.
'You damned whores, where are you? Quick, come here,
Dry this tobacco, fill a dozen of beer.
Will you be brief, or long you to be hanged?
Hold, take this match, go light it and be hanged.   20
Where stay these whores when gentlemen do call?
Here's no attendance, by the Lord, at all!'
   Then down the stairs the pots in rage he throws
And in a damned vein of swearing grows:

For he will challenge any under heaven
To swear with him, and give him six at seven.
Oh, he is an accomplished gentleman,
And many rare conceited knacks he can,
Which yield to him a greater store of gain
Than juggling kings, hey passe, legerdemain.   30
His wit's his living: one of quaint device,
For bowling-alleys, cockpits, cards or dice,
To those exploits he ever stands prepared,
A villain excellent at a bum-card.
The knave of clubs he any time can burn
And find him in his bosom, for his turn.
Tut, he hath cards for any kind of game,
Primero, saunt, or whatsoever name:
Make him but dealer, all his fellows swears
If you do find good dealing, take his ears.   40
But come to dice, why that's his only trade:
Michel Mumchance his own invention made.
He hath a stock whereon his living stays,
And they are fulhams and barred quarter-treys:
His langrets, with his high men and his low,
Are ready what his pleasure is to throw:
His stopped dice with quick-silver never miss,
He calls for 'Come on, five', and there it is:
Or else he'll have it with five and a reach
Although it cost his neck the halter-stretch.   50
   Besides all this same kind of cheating art,
The gentleman hath some other good part:
Well seen in magic and astrology,
Flinging a figure wondrous handsomely
Which, if it do not miss, it sure doth hit:
Of troth the man hath great store of small wit.
And note him, wheresoever that he goes
His book of characters is in his hose.
His dinner he will not presume to take
Ere he ask counsel of an almanack.   60
He'll find if one prove false unto his wife
Only with ox-blood and a rustic knife.
He can transform himself unto an ass,
Show you the Devil in a crystal-glass:

The Devil, say you? Why, aye: is that such wonder?
Being consorts, they will not be asunder.
Alchemy in his brains so sure doth settle,
He can make gold of any copper kettle:
Within a three weeks' space, or such a thing,
Riches upon the whole world he could bring.   70
But in his own purse one shall hardly spy it:
Witness his hostess, for a twelve-months' diet,
Who would be glad of gold, or silver either,
But swears by chalk and post, she can get neither.
    More, he will teach any to gain their love,
As thus: says he, 'Take me a turtle-dove,
And in an oven let her lie and bake
So dry that you may powder of her make;
Which being put into a cup of wine
The wench that drinks it will to love incline,   80
And shall not sleep in quiet in her bed
Till she be eased of her maidenhead.
This is *probatum*, and it hath been tried,
Or else the cunning man cunningly lied.'
It may be so, a lie is not so strange:
Perhaps he spake it when the moon did change
And thereupon, no doubt, the occasion sprung,
Unconstant Luna over-ruled his tongue.
Astronomers that traffic with the sky
By common censure sometimes meet the lie: 90
Although indeed their blame is not so much
When stars and planets fail and keep not touch.
And so this fellow with his large profession
That ends his trial in a far digression—
Philosophers bequeathed him their stone
To make gold with, yet can his purse hold none.

(*The Letting of Humour's Blood in the Head-Vein, Satire III*)

Melfluvious, sweet, rose-watered eloquence,
Thou that hast hunted barbarism hence
And taught the goodman Cobbin at his plough
To be as eloquent as Tully now:
Who nominicates his bread and cheese a name
That doth untruss the nature of the same—
His 'stomach-stayer': how d'ye like the phrase?
Are ploughmen simple fellows nowadays?
Not so, my masters! What means Singer then,
And Pope the clown, to speak so boorish, when   10
They counterfeit the clowns upon the stage,
Since country fellows grow in this same age
To be so quaint in their new printed speech,
That cloth will now compare with velvet breech?
Let him discourse even where and when he dare,
Talk ne'er so ink-horn learnedly and rare,
Swear cloth-breech is a peasant (by the Lord),
Threaten to draw his 'wrath-venger', his sword:
Tush, Cloth-breech doth deride him with a laugh
And lets him see 'bone-baster' (that's his staff);   20
Then tells him, 'Brother, friend or so forth, hear ye:
'Tis not your knitting-needle makes me fear ye.
If to ascension you are so declined,
I have a restitution in my mind:
For though your beard do stand so fine mustated,
Perhaps your nose may be transfisticated.
Man, I dare challenge thee to throw the sledge,
To jump or leap over a ditch or hedge,
To wrestle, play at stool-ball, or to run,
To pitch the bar, or to shoot off a gun,   30
To play at loggets, nine-holes or ten-pins,
To try it out at football by the shins;
At tick-tack, Irish, noddy, maw and ruff:
At hot-cockles, leap-frog or blind-man buff;
To drink half-pots or deal at the whole can,
To play at base, or pen and ink-horn Sir John:
To dance the Morris, play at barley-break:
At all exploits a man can think or speak:

At shove-groat, venter-point or cross and pile,
At "beshrew him who's last at yonder stile",   40
At leaping o'er a midsummer bonfire,
Or at the drawing Dun out of the mire:
At any of these or all these presently,
Wag but your finger, I am for you, I.
I scorn (that am a youngster of our town)
To let a Bow-bell cockney put me down.'
  This is a gallant far beyond a gull
For very valour fills his pockets full.
Wit showers upon him, wisdoms rain in plenty:
For he'll be hanged if any man find twenty   50
In all their parish, whatsoe'er they be,
Can show a head so politic as he.
It was his father's luck of late to die
Untestate; he about the legacy
To London came, enquiring all about
How he might find a civil villain out;
Being unto a civil lawyer sent,
'Pray sir', quoth he, 'are you the man I meant,
That have a certain kind of occupation
About dead men that leave things out of fashion?   60
Death hath done that which to answer he's not able:
My father he is died detestable;
I being his eldest heir, he did prefer
Me, sir, to be his executioner:
And very briefly my request to finish,
Pray, how may I by law his goods diminish?'
  Was this a clown? tell true, or was 'a none?
You make fat clowns, if such as he be one:
A man may swear, if he were urged to it,
Foolisher fellows have not so much wit.   70
Oh such as he are even the only men
Love-letters in a milk-maid's praise to pen:
Lines that will work the cursed'st sullen shrew
To love a man, whether she will or no,
Being most wonderous pathetical
To make Cis out a-cry in love withal.
He scorns that Master Schoolmaster should think
He wants his aid in half a pen of ink:

136

All that he doth, it cometh every whit
From nature's dry-fat, his own mother-wit.   80
As thus:
    'Thou honeysuckle of the hawthorn hedge,
Vouchsafe in Cupid's cup my heart to pledge:
My heart's dear blood, sweet Cis, is thy carouse,
Worth all the ale in Gammer Gubbins' house.
I say no more, affairs call me away:
My father's horse for provender doth stay.
Be thou the lady Cressid-light to me,
Sir Trollelolle I will prove to thee.
Written in haste: farewell, my cowslip sweet,   90
Pray let's a-Sunday at the ale-house meet.'

(*The Letting of Humour's Blood in the Head-Vein, Satire IV*)

32 · JOHN WEEVER

A Prophecy of this Present Year 1600

*. . . Who lives past ninety-nine
Shall afterwards speak of a blessed time*

Then cease fond satyres, quipping epigrammatists,
Sly scoffing critics, jeering Lucianists,
Stern censuring Catos, full-gorged Lucilians,
Envy-swollen Cynics, all-eyed Epidaurians,
Unringed routing hogs, otter-toothed Rhamnusians!
Cease, cease to bawl, thou wasp-stung satyrist,
Let none so testy-petulant insist!
Hold, stay thy lashing hand and jerking rhymes:
There is no lewdness in these halcyon times.
By heaven's powdered robe and fiery element,   10
There is no sin in Albion permanent.
Vice lies deep smothered in his darksome tomb
And virtue takes possession of his room:
All spotless pure, this first of Janivere,
Propitiously began great Plato's year;
Defer your rigorous envy-kindled rage
Until some other stranger sinning age;

Let hell-born sin with your untimely spite
Lie buried both in womb of silent night.
    Prophet (whosoe'er thou wert) heavens give thee meed   20
For this thy old-said saw and truest rede:
If I but knew where lay thy senseless urn,
Upon the same sweet odours I would burn
And solemnize thy dated exequies,
Hoping to be inspired with prophecies,
That so I might the veriment unfold
What happen us the next seven hundred should.
    In every nook and angle now I burst,
To all assemblies boldly do I thrust:
To Paul's, to plays, to prizes, revellings,   30
To dicing-houses, tavern-beverings,
To bowling-alleys, night-set merriments,
To Mile-end trainings, Tyburn dreriments,
To bear-baitings and every wonderment,
Each conduit-fray and little blunderment.
Enaunter some odd toyish fopperies
Should lie obscured from my searching eyes.
But 'mongst this rout I heard no foolish word
In serious earnest or in jesting bourd;
No scripture jests, no heaven-profaning oaths,   40
No sudden stabs, no French new-fangled clothes.
    Gallus hath left his new-stamped blasphemies,
Rubrine disclaims his damned heresies,
Writhled Silene his goatish bitchery
And Valodid his juggling witchery.
Bawdy Melino needs not lust relieve
With cordial compounds and preservative:
Rein-running botches, pocks, are voided clean.
Then Podelingus go and scrape again
In Florence stews with lustful Aretine: 50
Seal up your syringe, case up your implements,
Truss up your trinkets, Leuca's instruments
None use in jolting coaches hurried.
    Now Lucia looks like one twice buried,
Expecting hourly passage to her grave;
No muddy mind, no slimy dunghill-slave
But hates with Picthatch t' have his name defaced:

Vices are loathed and virtue is embraced.
'Give me a kingdom, Cynic: now I can
Show thee a complete rightly perfect man.'   60
    O wakeful prophet, that so far away
Could spy the dawning of this New-year's day!
And in thy true authentic prophecy
Foretell that brutish sensuality,
Leopard-skinned, soul-polluting sodomy,
Dogs' appetite, and damned impiety,
Should be transported into Italy
From England, this same year of jubilee.
    But tell me, satyres, now in seriousness
Why ripped ye forth the guts of viciousness   70
Or dipped your pens in puddle-beastliness?
It is dishonour and indignity
Unto a poet's great supremacy;
For, by the world's pure and immaculate
Self-yielding all-Saturnus maiden's state,
Not for a world of Indian treasury
Would I the world in terms so vilify,
Or prove it in my wrangling poesy
A broker's-shop of vile iniquity.
Nor should my lavish and malignant tongue   80
Tear out the bowels of sins hidden long,
Hook out abhorring-nature strange delights,
Drowned in the Dead Sea with the Sodomites:
For whilst such covered sins you do unveil,
Crabbed reprehension sets them but to sale.
    Not long ago (by chance) these ears of mine
O'erheard young Tusco read a satyre's line,
And gravelled (as it seemed) stood censuring,
His eyes fixed on a weather-cock, misconstruing
The gloomy sense, and 'sembled thereupon   90
Of frys and puisnes a convocation:
Slubbering the margent with their greasy thumbs
They found no means, till court-boy Brisco comes.
This agent-patient in a moment spied
Light in this dark line. Tusco then replied:
'I'm glad of this; I thought there had not been
Such novel pastimes, such a new-found sin.'

And since in Paul's I walking Tusco met,
And at his heels I saw young Brisco jet.
But by the spritely essence of my soul,   100
My retchless lines shall Brisco not control:
Nor rub the botch-sore on his ridden side,
Nor gird the galled blisters on his hide:
That would but more his grief exasperate
And all the world by him exulcerate.
Sin's like a puddle or a mattery sink:
The more we stir them, still the more they stink.
    O could the circuit of my pulsive brain
Harbour but in it such a Cynic strain,
I would have scourged self-blind Bravortian   110
Keeping in Newgate his lewd courtesan
So lusciously with sack and marrow-pies,
Whilst in the Fleet his uncle starving lies:
There fleet or sink or drown, his care is more
To snort in the arms of his shape-altering whore.
    When (for a coach) Malberia in a cart
Was jolted, then I crossed the streets athwart:
With rapiers pendant Minks and Mario ran
After this fat luxurious courtesan:
With draffy piss-pots still as she was crowned,   120
Minks wept for love, for anger Mario frowned.
This would have fazed a satyre's piss-steeped whip:
They 'scape my jerking rhyme or jocund quip.
    Though Cudro (not for kingdoms would I name him—
That were enough for evermore to shame him)
Maintain his servant, sister and his whore,
And yet maintain his sister and no more,
Should I unveil incestuous luxury?
Nay, rather curtain-o'er such brothelry!
    Though Vicro bezzle on the ale-house bench   130
Till 's jacket's bawdy with the barmy drench,
And thereupon unto his audience preach,
At every full-point ysking forth a belch,
Slupping the chalice like a drunken scale
Where frothy lamb's-wool swims in nappy ale;
And thence return and guzzle off the bowl
Till 's eyes 'gan startle in his jobbernoll.

140

Though Dario brag that for reward or fee
He never made his muse a mercenary;
Yet written gives her unto noble men   140
And in exchange receives their angels then.
   Though Lacrion in a bravery disburse
For jingling spurs the jingling of his purse—
He spurs not me, nor do his rowels prick:
And wherefore then 'gainst Lacrion should I kick?
Why should I Dario's brag reiterate
Or damned Vicro's vice exaggerate?
   Burno exclaimed, as Cicero wont to cry
When Catiline did work conspiracy,
'O times, o manners lewd and impious',   150
When his own manners made the time so vicious.
What beastliness by others you have shown,
Such by yourselves 'tis thought that you have known.
But vice, this year of virtue, makes an end:
Ill at the worst doth always 'gin to mend.

33 · NICHOLAS BRETON

A Solemn Farewell to the World

Oh forlorn Fancy, whereto dost thou live
To weary out the senses with unrest?
Hopes are but cares, that but discomforts give,
While only fools do climb the phoenix' nest:
To heart-sick souls all joys are but a jest.
   Thou dost in vain but strive against the stream,
   With blinded eyes to see the sunny beam.

Die with desire, abandoned from delight.
Thy weary winter lasteth all the year.
Say to thyself that darkness is the light,   10
Wherein doth nothing but thy death appear;
While wit and sense, in sorrow's heavy cheer,
   Finds thee an humour but unkindly bred
   Of Hope's illusions, in too weak a head.

Fortune affrights thee with a thousand fears,
While folly feeds thee with abuse of wit;
And while thy force in fainting passion wears
Patience is ready to increase the fit,
Where agonies in their extremes do sit:
   So that each way thy soul is so perplexed   20
   As better die than live to be so vexed.

Say, patience somewhat do assuage thy pain;
Prolonged cures are too uncomfortable;
And where that care doth never comfort gain,
The state, alas, must needs be miserable.
Where sorrow's labours are so lamentable,
   That silence says, that to the soul complains,
   Concealed sorrows are the killing pains.

Then do not cease to sigh and sob thy fill,
Bleed in the tears of true love's living blood;   30
Show how unkindness seeks the heart to kill,
That hides a buzzard in a falcon's hood:
Feed not thyself with misconceited good;
   Better to starve than in a sugared pill
   To taste the poison of the spirit's ill.

But if thou canst content thee with thy life,
And wilt endure a double death to live;
If thou canst bear that bitter kind of strife
Where cross conceits but discontents do give;
If to this end thou canst thine humour drive,   40
   And care's true patience can command thee so,
   Give me then leave to tell thee what I know.

I know too well, that all too long have tried,
That earth containeth not that may content thee;
Sorrow will so beset thee on each side,
That wit nor reason can the thought invent thee
But that will some way serve for to torment thee.
   Hope will deceive thee, happiness go by thee,
   Fortune will fail thee and the world defy thee.

Beauty will blind thine eyes, bewitch thine heart,   50
Confound thy senses and command thy will,
Scorn thy desire, not look on thy desert,
Disdain thy service, quite thy good with ill,
And make no care thy very soul to kill:
   Time will outgo thee, sorrow overtake thee,
   And death a shadow of a substance make thee.

I know this world will never be for thee:
Conscience must carry thee another way.
Another world must be for thee and me,
Where happy thoughts must make their holiday,   60
While heavenly comforts never will decay.
   We must not think in this ill age to thrive
   Where Faith and Love are scarcely found alive.

We must not build our houses on the sands,
Where every flood will wash them quite away:
Nor set our seals unto those wicked bands,
Where damned souls their debts in hell must pay;
Our states must stand upon a better stay:
   Upon the rock we must our houses build,
   That will our frames from wind and water shield.   70

Go, bid the world, with all his trash, farewell,
And tell the earth it shall be all but dust:
These wicked wares that worldlings buy and sell
The moth will eat or else the canker rust.
All flesh is grass and to the grave it must.
   This sink of sin is but the way to hell;
   Leave it, I say, and bid the world farewell.

Account of pomp but as a shadowed power,
And think of friends but as the summer flies;
Esteem of beauty as a fading flower   80
And lovers' fancies but as fabled lies:
Know that on earth there is no Paradise.
   Who sees not heaven is surely spirit-blind
   And like a body that doth lack a mind.

Then let us lie as dead, till there we live,
Where only love doth live for ever blest;
And only love the only life doth give,
That brings the soul unto eternal rest:
Let us this wicked, wretched world detest,
    Where graceless hearts in hellish sins persever,
    And fly to heaven, to live in grace for ever.   91

34 · RICHARD MIDDLETON

Time's Metamorphosis

Tempora mutantur et nos mutamur in illis

Time changeth still, and we are changed with time: 373
And I have changed the method of my rhyme
To a more general critique. Who can contain
His patient'st wit within a silent strain
That sees Pandulpho's pride, attorney's gown,
Wave with the wanton wind? Himself a clown
Swaddled in self-opinion, but in sense
(If brought to proof) an infant? Get thee hence,   380
Pygmy-attorney, actor, Christmas-player:
I scorn to seat thee in my verse's chair.
But what is he of such a brazen sense,
Object opinion, dulled with his offence,
That sees and duly marks the vacillation
Of Stadius' mind, his usury-transmigration?
Fulvius' lascivious habit, pride and gesture?
Licinius' perjury? Tatius' pilfered vesture?
Pharmacus' feigned devotion, fond preciseness?
Pantalia's luxury and admired niceness—   390
Her 'Fie, nay, fie, away, what do you mean?
Think you my state shall warrant me a quean?'
Who would not think, that sees Flaminius brawling,
Quintius revolted and Tarquinius falling
From true religion, but that heaven's great frame
Should scatter thunderbolts to ding the same

Unto eternal darkness? or that the earth
Should even have swallowed all these at their birth.
Who with their several crimes are so wrapped in
By time's swift change, sin is with them no sin.   400
I hate my aspiring muse should once descend
To mark the base employment, or attend
To character the humours of Foenor's son,
Strutting Fraudento, whose impression
Is so far discrepant from modesty
As it is next to pride and foolery.
I scorn to write of every lawyer's lad
Who like some of our new-dubbed knights are clad,
And jet with such presumption in the street,
They'll not vail bonnet to the best they meet.   410
   Great change of time: o time's impurity,
When such base slaves assume gentility!
Yet for their pride (and that doth bring the loathing)
They're Aesop's apes, tricked up in costly clothing,
'Mongst whom, being taught to dance, mask, walk upright—
Wherein the lookers-on took great delight—
A learned philosopher did scatter nuts:
Then they left dancing, fell to feed their guts;
So their base offsprings, asses in their gestures,
Painted like apes, and images in their vestures,   420
Do what they can, sweeten themselves with fumes,
They're but black crows decked with the peacock's plumes.
   And now at last time's metamorphosis
Concords now with my rhyme's antiphrasis.
A satyr lately, now in mildy style
I meditate and muse, and musing smile,
To think how the readers will conceit my verse
Wherein paraphrased I do rehearse
Time's objects, men in time's conformity,
Changed into villainous enormity.   430
Saith one, 'he lacks his wits and wants his senses
To write of nothing but of men's offences'.
'O', saith another, 'he is too too plain,
He doth not use a critic poet's vein;'
'He describes men too large', the third doth say:
'Then why should we his harsh invectives weigh?'

And troth, the last opinion (in my sense)
Deserves best praise: why should men take offence,
To read their own intemperate vice portrayed
When others to their teeth their faults upbraid? 440
But every man will have a several censure
To wrest my verses with a false conjecture
'Gainst the intention. No, judicious spirits!
I envy no man or malign their merits.
Such bitter stinging gall was never mix'd
With pureness of my style, nor have I fix'd
My humble muse upon so high a pin
That it should scourge the world, publish all's sin.
This I protest, and I will stand unto it:
'Twas no malignant fury made me do it, 450
But 'twas the revolutions of these times,
And men's retrogradians, made these rhymes.

35 · BEN JONSON

Horace, Satires, II, i

Horace   There are, to whom I seem excessive sour
And past a satyre's law to extend my power:
Others that think whatever I have writ
Wants pith and matter to eternise it,
And that they could in one day's light disclose
A thousand verses such as I compose.
What shall I do, Trebatius? Say.
Trebatius   Surcease.
Horace   And shall my muse admit no more increase?
Trebatius So I advise.
Horace   An ill death let me die
If 'twere not best; but sleep avoids mine eye 10
And I use these lest nights should tedious seem.
Trebatius Rather contend to sleep, and live like them
That, holding golden sleep in special price,
Rubbed with sweet oils swim silver Tiber thrice
And every even with neat wine steeped be.
Or, if such love of writing ravish thee,

	Then dare to sing unconquered Caesar's deeds,	
	Who cheers such actions with abundant meeds.	
Horace	That, father, I desire; but when I try	
	I feel defects in every faculty:	20
	Nor is't a labour fit for every pen,	
	To paint the horrid troops of armed men,	
	The lances burst in Gallia's slaughtered forces	
	Or wounded Parthians tumbled from their horses:	
	Great Caesar's wars cannot be fought with words.	
Trebatius	Yet what his virtue in his peace affords,	
	His fortitude and justice, thou canst show	
	As wise Lucilius honoured Scipio.	
Horace	Of that, my powers shall suffer no neglect	
	When such slight labours may inspire respect:	30
	But if I watch not a most chosen time	
	The humble words of Flaccus cannot climb	
	The attentive ear of Caesar; nor must I	
	With less observance shun gross flattery:	
	For he, reposed safe in his own merit,	
	Spurns back the gloses of a fawning spirit.	
Trebatius	But how much better would such accents sound,	
	Than with a sad and serious verse to wound	
	Pantolabus railing in his saucy jests	
	Or Nomentanus spent in riotous feasts?	40
	In satyres, each man, though untouched, complains	
	As he were hurt, and hates such biting strains.	
Horace	What shall I do? Milonius shakes his heels	
	In ceaseless dances when his brain once feels	
	The stirring fervour of the wine ascend;	
	And that his eyes false numbers apprehend.	
	Castor his horse, Pollux loves handy-fights;	
	A thousand heads, a thousand choice delights.	
	My pleasure is, in feet my words to close,	
	As (both our better) old Lucilius does.	50
	He as his trusty friends his books did trust	
	With all his secrets; nor in things unjust	
	Or actions lawful ran to other men.	
	So that the old man's life, described, was seen	
	As in a votive tablet, in his lines.	
	And to his steps my genius inclines,	

Lucanian or Apulian I not whether
(For the Venusian colony ploughs either,
Sent thither when the Sabines were forced thence,
As old fame sings, to give the place defence   60
'Gainst such as, seeing it empty, might make road
Upon the empire, or there fix abode:
Whether the Apulian borderer it were
Or the Lucanian violence they fear).

But this my style no living man shall touch
If first I be not forced by base reproach;
But, like a sheathed sword, it shall defend
My innocent life; for why should I contend
To draw it out, when no malicious thief
Robs my good name, the treasure of my life?   70
O Jupiter, let it with rust be eaten
Before it touch or insolently threaten
The life of any with the least disease;
So much I love and woo a general peace.
But he that wrongs me, better (I proclaim)
He never had assayed to touch my fame:
For he shall weep and walk with every tongue
Throughout the city, infamously sung.
Servius the praetor threats the laws and urn
If any at his deeds repine or spurn;   80
The witch Canidia, that Albutius got,
Denounceth witchcraft where she loveth not;
Thurius the judge doth thunder worlds of ill
To such as strive with his judicial will.
All men affright their foes in what they may:
Nature commands it, and men must obey.

Observe with me: the wolf doth his tooth use,
The bull his horn. And who doth this infuse
But nature? There's luxurious Scaeva; trust
His long-lived mother with him: his so just   90
And scrupulous right hand no mischief will,
Nor more than with his heel a wolf with kill
Or ox with jaw. Marry, let him alone
With tempered poison to remove the crone.

But briefly, if to age I destined be,
Or that quick death's black wings environ me;

If rich or poor; at Rome; or fate command
I shall be banished to some other land:
What hue soever my whole state shall bear,
I will write satyres still, in spite of fear.   100

Trebatius   Horace, I fear thou draw'st no lasting breath,
And that some great man's friend will be thy death.

Horace   What? when the man that first did satyrize
Durst pull the skin over the ears of vice
And make who stood in outward fashion clear
Give place, as foul within,—shall I forbear?
Did Laelius, or the man so great with fame
That from sacked Carthage fetched his worthy
          name,
Storm, that Lucilius did Metellus pierce?
Or bury Lupus quick in famous verse?   110
Rulers and subjects by whole tribes he checked,
But virtue and her friends did still protect:
And when from sight or from the judgment-seat
The virtuous Scipio and wise Laelius met,
Unbraced, with him in all light sports they shared
Till their most frugal suppers were prepared.
Whate'er I am, though both for wealth and wit
Beneath Lucilius I am pleased to sit,
Yet envy, spite of her empoisoned breast,
Shall say I lived in grace here with the best: 120
And seeking in weak trash to make her wound,
Shall find me solid, and her teeth unsound:
'Less learned Trebatius' censure disagree.

Trebatius No, Horace; I of force must yield to thee;
Only take heed, as being advised by me,
Lest thou incur some danger: better pause
Than rue thy ignorance of the sacred laws.
There's justice; and great action may be sued
'Gainst such as wrong men's fame with verses lewd.

Horace   Ay, with lewd verses, such as libels be   130
And aimed at persons of good quality:
I reverence and adore that just decree.
But if they shall be sharp yet modest rhymes
That spare men's persons and but tax their crimes,
Such shall in open court find current pass

Were Caesar judge, and with the maker's grace.
Trebatius Nay, I'll add more; if thou thyself being clear
Shalt tax in person a man fit to bear
Shame and reproach, his suit shall quickly be
Dissolved in laughter, and thou thence set free.   140

36 · BEN JONSON

Inviting a Friend to Supper

Tonight, grave sir, both my poor house and I
Do equally desire your company:
Not that we think us worthy such a guest,
But that your worth will dignify our feast
With those that come, whose grace may make that seem
Something, which else could hope for no esteem.
It is the fair acceptance, sir, creates
The entertainment perfect, not the cates.
Yet shall you have, to rectify your palate,
An olive, capers, or some better salad   10
Ushering the mutton, with a short-legged hen
(If we can get her) full of eggs, and then
Lemons and wine for sauce; to these, a cony
Is not to be despaired of, for our money;
And though fowl now be scarce, yet there are clerks,
The skies not falling, think we may have larks.
   I'll tell you more, and lie, so you will come—
Of partridge, pheasant, woodcock, of which some
May yet be there, and godwit, if we can,
Knat, rail and ruff too. Howsoe'er, my man   20
Shall read a piece of Virgil, Tacitus,
Livy, or of some better book to us,
Of which we'll speak our minds amidst our meat;
And I'll profess no verses to repeat.
To this, if aught appear which I not know of,
That will the pastry, not my paper, show of.
Digestive cheese and fruit there sure will be;
But that which most doth take my Muse and me

Is a pure cup of rich Canary wine,
Which is the Mermaid's now, but shall be mine: 30
Of which had Horace or Anacreon tasted,
Their lives, as do their lines, till now had lasted.
Tobacco, nectar or the Thespian spring
Are all but Luther's beer to this I sing.
Of this we will sup free, but moderately,
And we will have no Poley or Parrot by,
Nor shall our cups make any guilty men;
But at our parting we will be as when
We innocently met. No simple word
That shall be uttered at our mirthful board 40
Shall make us sad next morning, or affright
The liberty that we'll enjoy tonight.

37 · BEN JONSON

On the Famous Voyage

No more let Greece her bolder fables tell
Of Hercules, or Theseus going to hell;
Orpheus; Ulysses; or the Latin muse
With tales of Troy's just knight our faiths abuse.
We have a Shelton and a Heyden got
Had power to act what they to feign had not.
All that they boast of Styx, of Acheron,
Cocytus, Phlegethon, our have proved in one—
The filth, stench, noise—save only what was there
Subtly distinguished, was confused here. 10
Their wherry had no sail, too; ours had none:
And in it two more horrid knaves than Charon.
Arses were heard to croak instead of frogs,
And for one Cerberus the whole coast was dogs.
Furies there wanted not: each scold was ten.
And, for the cries of ghosts, women and men,
Laden with plague-sores, and their sins, were heard:
Lashed by their consciences, to die afeared.
Then let the former age with this content her:
She brought the poets forth, but ours the adventure. 20

I sing the brave adventures of two wights,
And pity 'tis I cannot call 'em knights:
One was, and he for brawn and brain right able
To have been styled of King Arthur's table.
The other was a squire of fair degree,
But in the action, greater man than he:
Who gave, to take at his return from hell,
His three for one. Now, lordings, listen well.
   It was the day, what time the powerful moon
Makes the poor Bankside creature wet its shoon   10
In its own hall; when these (in worthy scorn
Of those that put out moneys on return
From Venice, Paris or some inland passage
Of six times to and fro without embassage—
Of him that backward went to Berwick, or which
Did dance the famous morris unto Norwich)—
At Bread-street's Mermaid, having dined, and merry,
Proposed to go to Holborn in a wherry:
A harder task than either his to Bristo'
Or his to Antwerp. Therefore once more, list ho!   20
   A dock there is, that called is Avernus—
Of some, Bride-well—and may in time concern us
All, that are readers: but, methinks, 'tis odd
That all this while I have forgot some god
Or goddess to invoke, to stuff my verse,
And with both bombard-style and phrase rehearse
The many perils of this port; and how,
Sans help of Sibyl or a golden bough
Or magic sacrifice, they passed along!
Alcides, be thou succouring to my song: 30
Thou hast seen hell (some say) and know'st all nooks there,
Canst tell me best how every Fury looks there;
And art a god, if fame thee not abuses,
Always at hand to aid the merry muses.
Great Club-fist, though thy back and bones be sore
Still with thy former labours, yet once more
Act a brave work, call it thy last adventry.
But hold my torch, while I describe the entry

152

To this dire passage. Say, thou stop thy nose:
'Tis but light pains. Indeed, this dock's no rose.   40
    In the first jaws appeared that ugly monster
Ycleped Mud, which when their oars did once stir
Belched forth an air as hot as at a muster
Of all your night-tubs, when the carts do cluster,
Who shall discharge first his merd-urinous load.
Thorough her womb they make their famous road
Between two walls: where, on one side, to scar men,
Were seen your ugly Centaurs ye call car-men,
Gorgonian scolds and Harpies; on the other
Hung stench, diseases and old filth, their mother,   50
With famine, wants and sorrows many a dozen,
The least of which was to the plague a cousin.
But they unfrighted pass, though many a privy
Spake to 'em louder than the ox in Livy,
And many a sink poured out her rage anenst 'em,
But still their virtue and their valour fenced 'em
And on they went, like Castor brave and Pollux,
Ploughing the main; when, see (the worst of all lucks)
They met the second prodigy, would fear a
Man that had never heard of a Chimaera.   60
One said 'twas the bold Briareus or the beadle
(Who hath the hundred hands when he doth meddle);
The other thought it Hydra, or the rock
Made of the trull that cut her father's lock:
But coming near they found it but a lighter,
So huge, it seemed, they could by no means quite her.
'Back', cried their brace of Charons; they cried 'No,
No going back! On still, you rogues, and row.'
'How hight the place?' A voice was heard: 'Cocytus.'
'Row close, then, slaves.' 'Alas, they will beshite us!'   70
'No matter stinkards, row.' 'What croaking sound
Is this we hear? of frogs?' 'No, guts, wind-bound,
Over your heads. Well, row.' At this, a loud
Crack did report itself, as if a cloud
Had burst with storm, and down fell, *ab excelsis*,
Poor Mercury, crying on Paracelsus
And all his followers, that had so abused him
And in so shitten sort so long had used him.

For (where he was the god of eloquence
And subtlety of metals) they dispense
His spirits, now in pills and eke in potions,
Suppositories, cataplasms and lotions.
'But many moons there shall not wane' (quoth he)
—In the meantime let 'em imprison me—
But I will speak, and know I shall be heard,
Touching this cause, where they will be afeared
To answer me. 'And sure, it was th' intent
Of the grave fart late let in Parliament,
Had it been seconded, and not in fume
Vanished away: as you must all presume
Their Mercury did now. By this, the stem
Of the hulk touched, and as by Polypheme
The sly Ulysses stole in a sheep's skin,
The well-greased wherry now had got between,
And bade her farewell sough unto the lurden:
Never did bottom more betray her burden.
The meat-boats of Bears' college, Paris-garden,
Stunk not so ill; nor, when she kissed, Kate Arden.
Yet one day in the year for sweet 'tis voiced,
And that is when it is the Lord Mayor's foist.
   By this time they had reached the Stygian pool,
By which the Masters swear when, on the stool
Of worship, they their nodding chins do hit
Against their breasts. Here, several ghosts did flit
About the shore, of farts but late departed,
White, black, blue, green, and in more forms out-started
Than all those atomi ridiculous
Whereof old Democrite and Hill (Nicholas)
One said, the other swore, the world consists.
These be the cause of those thick frequent mists
Arising in that place, through which who goes
Must try the unused valour of a nose;
And that ours did. For, yet, no nare was tainted,
Nor thumb, nor finger to the stop acquainted,
But open and unarmed encountered all:
Whether it languishing stuck upon the wall
Or were precipitated down the jakes
And, after, swum abroad in ample flakes;

Or that it lay heaped like an usurer's mass:
All was to them the same, they were to pass,   120
And so they did, from Styx to Acheron,
The ever-boiling flood: whose banks upon,
Your Fleet-lane Furies and hot cooks do dwell
That with still-scalding steams make the place hell.
The sinks ran grease, and hair of measled hogs,
The heads, houghs, entrails and the hides of dogs:
For, to say truth, what scullion is so nasty
To put the skins and offal in a pasty?
Cats there lay divers had been flayed and roasted,
And, after mouldy grown, again were toasted: 130
Then, selling not, a dish was ta'en to mince 'em,
But still it seemed the rankness did convince 'em.
For here they were thrown in with the melted pewter,
Yet drowned they not. They had five lives in future.
   But 'mongst these Tiberts, who d'you think there was?
Old Banks the juggler, our Pythagoras,
Grave tutor to the learned horse: both which
Being, beyond sea, burned for one witch,
Their spirits transmigrated to a cat:
And now above the pool a face right fat,   140
With great grey eyes, are lifted up, and mewed:
Thrice did it spit, thrice dived. At last it viewed
Our brave heroes with a milder glare
And, in a piteous tune, began. 'How dare
Your dainty nostrils (in so hot a season,
When every clerk eats artichokes and peason,
Laxative lettuce and such windy meats)
Tempt such a passage? When each privy seat
Is filled with buttock, and the walls do sweat
Urine and plasters? When the noise doth beat   150
Upon your ears of discords so unsweet,
And outcries of the damned in the Fleet?
Cannot the Plague-bill keep you back, nor bells
Of loud Sepulchre's with their hourly knells,
But you will visit grisly Pluto's hall?
Behold where Cerberus, reared on the wall
Of Holborn (three sergeants' heads) looks o'er
And stays but till you come unto the door!

155

Tempt not his fury: Pluto is away,
And Madame Caesar, great Proserpina,   160
Is now from home. You lose your labours quite,
Were you Jove's sons, or had Alcides' might.
   They cried out 'Puss!' He told them he was Banks
That had so often showed 'em merry pranks.
They laughed at his laugh-worthy fate, and passed
The triple head without a sop. At last,
Calling for Rhadamanthus that dwelt by,
A soap-boiler; and Aeacus him nigh,
Who kept an ale-house; with my little Minos,
An ancient purblind fletcher with a high nose—   170
They took 'em all to witness of their action,
And so went bravely back without protraction.
   In memory of which most liquid deed
The city since hath raised a pyramid.
And I could wish for their eternized sakes,
My muse had ploughed with his that sung A-JAX.

38 · BEN JONSON

To Penshurst

Thou art not, Penshurst, built to envious show,
Of touch, or marble; nor canst boast a row
Of polished pillars, or a roof of gold:
Thou hast no lantern whereof tales are told,
Or stair, or courts: but stand'st an ancient pile,
And these grudged at, art reverenced the while.
Thou joy'st in better marks: of soil, of air,
Of wood, of water; therein thou art fair.
Thou hast thy walks for health as well as sport:
Thy mount to which the dryads do resort,   10
Where Pan and Bacchus their high feasts have made
Beneath the broad beech and the chestnut shade:
That taller tree which of a nut was set
At his great birth where all the Muses met.
There, in the writhed bark, are cut the names
Of many a sylvan taken with his flames.

And thence the ruddy satyrs oft provoke
The lighter fauns to reach thy lady's oak.
Thy copse too, named of Gamage, thou hast there,
That never fails to serve thee seasoned deer   20
When thou wouldst feast or exercise thy friends.
  The lower land, that to the river bends,
Thy sheep, thy bullocks, kine and calves do feed:
The middle grounds thy mares and horses breed.
Each bank doth yield thee coneys; and the tops
Fertile of wood, Ashour and Sidney's copse,
To crown thy open table, doth provide
The purpled pheasant with the speckled side;
The painted partridge lies in every field
And for thy mess is willing to be killed.   30
  And if the high-swollen Medway fail thy dish,
Thou hast thy ponds that pay thee tribute fish:
Fat, aged carps that run into thy net,
And pikes, now weary their own kind to eat,
As loth the second draught or cast to stay,
Officiously at first themselves betray.
Bright eels that emulate them and leap on land
Before the fisher, or into his hand.
  Then hath thy orchard fruit, thy garden flowers
Fresh as the air and new as are the hours.   40
The early cherry, with the later plum,
Fig, grape and quince, each in his time doth come;
The blushing apricot and woolly peach
Hang on thy walls, that every child may reach.
And though thy walls be of the country stone,
They are reared with no man's ruin, no man's groan.
There's none that dwell about them wish them down,
But all come in, the farmer and the clown,
And no one empty-handed, to salute
Thy lord and lady, though they have no suit.   50
Some bring a capon, some a rural cake,
Some nuts, some apples; some, that think they make
The better cheeses, bring 'em, or else send
By their ripe daughters, whom they would commend
This way to husbands, and whose baskets bear
An emblem of themselves in plum or pear.

But what can this (more than express their love)
Add to thy free provisions, far above
The needs of such? whose liberal board doth flow
With all that hospitality doth know!   60
Where comes no guest but is allowed to eat
Without his fear, and of the lord's own meat:
Where the same beer and bread, and self-same wine
That is his lordship's shall be also mine.
And I not fain to sit (as some this day
At great men's tables) and yet dine away.
Here no man tells my cups; nor, standing by,
A waiter doth my gluttony envy,
But gives me what I want and lets me eat:
He knows below he shall find plenty of meat.   70
Thy tables hoard not up for the next day,
Nor when I take my lodging need I pray
For fire or lights or livery: all is there,
As if thou then wert mine or I reigned here:
There's nothing I can wish for which I stay.
That found King James, when hunting late this way
With his brave son, the Prince: they saw thy fires
Shine bright on every hearth as the desires
Of thy Penates had been set on flame
To entertain them; or the country came   80
With all their zeal to warm their welcome here.
What—great I will not say, but sudden—cheer
Didst thou then make 'em! and what praise was heaped
On thy good lady then, who therein reaped
The just reward of her high housewifery:
To have her linen, plate and all things nigh
When she was far, and not a room but dressed
As if it had expected such a guest!
    These, Penshurst, are thy praise, and yet not all.
Thy lady's noble, fruitful, chaste withal.   90
His children thy great lord may call his own:
A fortune in this age but rarely known.
They are, and have been taught religion: thence
Their gentler spirits have sucked innocence.
Each morn and even they are taught to pray
With the whole household, and may every day

158

Read in their virtuous parents' noble parts
The mysteries of manners, arms and arts.
Now, Penshurst, they that will proportion thee
With other edifices, when they see   100
Those proud, ambitious heaps and nothing else,
May say their lords have built, but thy lord dwells.

39 · BEN JONSON

To Sir Robert Wroth

How blest art thou, canst love the country, Wroth,
    Whether by choice, or fate, or both;
And though so near the city and the court
    Art ta'en with neither's vice nor sport:
That at great times art no ambitious guest
    Of sheriff's dinner or mayor's feast.
Nor com'st to view the better cloth of state,
    The richer hangings or crown-plate;
Nor throng'st (when masquing is) to have a sight
    Of the short bravery of the night,   10
To view the jewels, stuffs, the pains, the wit
    There wasted, some not paid for yet!
But canst at home in thy securer rest
    Live, with unbought provisions blest;
Free from proud porches or their gilded roofs
    'Mongst lowing herds and solid hoofs
Alongst the curled woods and painted meads,
    Through which a serpent river leads
To some cool courteous shade which he calls his,
    And makes sleep softer than it is!   20
Or if thou list the night in watch to break,
    Abed canst hear the loud stag speak
In spring, oft roused for his master's sport,
    Who, for it, makes thy house his court;
Or with thy friends the heart of all the year
    Divid'st upon the lesser deer;
In autumn at the partridge makes a flight
    And giv'st thy gladder guests the sight;

And in the winter hunt'st the flying hare
    More for thy exercise than fare,   30
While all that follow, their glad ears apply
    To the full greatness of the cry;
Or hawking at the river or the bush,
    Or shooting at the greedy thrush
Thou dost with some delight the day outwear
    Although the coldest of the year!
The whilst, the several seasons thou has seen
    Of flowery fields, of copses green,
The mowed meadows with the fleeced sheep,
    And feasts that either shearers keep;   40
The ripened ears yet humble in their height,
    And furrows laden with their weight;
The apple-harvest that doth longer last,
    The hogs returned home fat from mast;
The trees cut out in log, and those boughs made
    A fire now, that lent a shade!
Thus Pan and Sylvane having had their rites,
    Comus puts in for new delights,
And fills thy open hall with mirth and cheer
    As if in Saturn's reign it were.   50
Apollo's harp and Hermes' lyre resound;
    Nor are the muses strangers found.
The rout of rural folk come thronging in
    (Their rudeness then is thought no sin),
Thy noblest spouse affords them welcome grace,
    And the great heroes of her race
Sit mixed with loss of state or reverence:
    Freedom doth with degree dispense.
The jolly wassail walks the often round
    And in their cups their cares are drowned.   60
They think not then which side the cause shall leese,
    Nor how to get the lawyer fees.
Such, and no other, was that age of old
    Which boasts t' have had the head of gold:
And such since thou canst make thine own content,
    Strive, Wroth, to live long innocent.
Let others watch in guilty arms, and stand
    The fury of a rash command,

Go enter breaches, meet the cannon's rage,
  That they may sleep with scars in age,   70
And show their feathers shot and colours torn,
  And brag that they were therefore born.
Let this man sweat and wrangle at the bar
  For every price, in every jar,
And change possessions oftener with his breath
  Than either money, war or death;
Let him than hardest sires more disinherit,
  And each-where boast it as his merit
To blow up orphans, widows, and their states,
  And think his power doth equal Fate's.   80
Let that go heap a mass of wretched wealth
  Purchased by rapine, worse than stealth,
And brooding o'er it sit with broadest eyes,
  Not doing good, scarce when he dies.
Let thousands more go flatter vice and win
  By being organs to great sin;
Get place and honour, and be glad to keep
  The secrets that shall break their sleep.
And so they ride in purple, eat in plate,
  Though poison, think it a great fate.   90
But thou, my Wroth, if I can truth apply,
  Shalt neither that nor this envy:
Thy peace is made; and when man's state is well,
  'Tis better, if he there can dwell.
God wisheth none should wrack on a strange shelf:
  To Him man's dearer than to himself.
And whosoever we may think things sweet,
  He always gives what He knows meet,
Which who can use is happy: such be thou.
  Thy morning's and thy evening's vow   100
Be thanks to Him, and earnest prayer to find
  A body sound, with sounder mind;
To do thy country service, thyself right,
  That neither want do thee affright
Nor death: but when thy latest sand is spent
  Thou may'st think life a thing but lent.

NOTES

1. See Introduction, p. 13. This anonymous satirical burlesque of *The Ship of Fools* was probably written not long after 1506. Though indebted to Chaucer, it gives an authentic picture of low life in London at the beginning of the sixteenth century. 'Cock Lorell' is probably a type-name (lorel = losel, rogue); he became a legendary anti-hero (see John Awdeley's *Fraternity of Vagabonds*, 1565). The poem is a fragment of 414 lines, the beginning being lost in the surviving copy printed by Wynkyn de Worde (in the British Museum: reprinted with the original spelling for the Percy Society, 1843). See also S. M. Tucker, *Verse Satire in England Before the Renaissance*, pp. 177–80.

49. *Coulter log.* Piece of wood to which the knife was attached.

55. *Gong-farmer.* Privy-cleaner.

56. *Masser-scourer.* Scavenger.

57. *Channel.* Gutter. Cf. **23**, 48.

59. *Henkam.* Henbane.

64. *Tollers.* Those who take toll: see 76.

65. *Pickers.* Thieves.

71. Cf. Chaucer's Miller, *Prologue*, A 560–6.

76. *Tolled.* Cf. Chaucer, loc. cit., 'well could he stealen corn and tollen thrice'. In addition to his payment for grinding corn, the miller took his share or 'toll' of the corn he ground.

83. *Quarterage.* Payment (of their fare).

89. *Maintenance again right.* Medieval legal formula: the action of wrongfully aiding litigants against justice.

92. *Clatterer.* Gossip.

96. *Leasing.* Lies.

97. *Boller.* Drunkard.

100. *A-Christ's corse, gatherer.* Of Corpus Christi, tax-collector.

160. Refers to the temporary closing of the Southwark stews (brothels) in 1506, recorded in the Great Chronicle of London. The bishop of Winchester, who had a house in Southwark, administered the stews under a statute of Henry II. See *Stow's Survey of London*, ed. C. L. Kingsford (1908), ii, 55, 366.

163. *Saint Katherine's.* See note on 170.

170. 'The parish church of St Katherine called Coleman, which addition … was taken of a great Haw yard or garden … called Coleman haw (haw = hedge).' (*Stow's Survey of London*, i, 149.)

172. *'n'.* I have so printed the original reading 'and' (= than). *The half-street.* One of the streets off Bankside where the stews were.

184. The pardoner's trade was notorious: cf. **7** and the notes on Chaucer's Pardoner in *The Complete Poems of Geoffrey Chaucer*, ed. F. N. Robinson (Oxford, 1933), pp. 667, 729.

194. *Dirige.* Dirge: from the first word of the Latin text of Psalm 5.8, used as an antiphon in the Roman Catholic Office of the Dead.

354. *Borrow.* Defend (ironical).

358. *Peal.* Salute.

364. *Try.* Select.

382. *Sperus.* Hesperus.

390. *Saint Julian's turn.* A 'turn' is the place where a river bends. St Julian, patron saint of hospitality, was said to have set up a 'hospital' at a ford where he gave free board and lodging as a penance for having accidentally killed his parents: see *The Complete Works of Geoffrey Chaucer*, ed. W. W. Skeat (1894–7), iii, 265.

395. *Mow.* Jest. *Stir.* Make a disturbance. The satirist's role here is still largely 'Goliardic'.

398. *Charterers.* Carthusians. *Innholders.* Innkeepers.

410. Every third person in England is a knave.

2. See Introduction, pp. 11–12. John Skelton, clerk in holy orders and 'poet laureate' (then a University title), died in 1529. *Colin Clout*, probably written in 1522, is a long satire against the clergy with covert attacks on the powers of an unnamed prelate (Wolsey). The standard complete edition is *The Poetical Works of John Skelton*, ed. A. Dyce (2 vols., 1843) with monumental commentary. The modernized text by P. Henderson (reprinted 1959) has inadequate notes and is textually unreliable. The best recent selection (including extracts from *Colin Clout*) is by R. S. Kinsman (Clarendon Medieval and Tudor series, 1969): his text differs slightly from that here printed. See also W. Nelson, 'Skelton's Quarrel with Wolsey', *PMLA*, li (1936), 377–98; W. Nelson, *John Skelton, Laureate* (reprinted New York, 1964), pp. 185–211; A. Heiserman, *Skelton and Satire* (Chicago, 1961), pp. 190–243; R. S. Kinsman, 'The Voices of Dissonance', *Huntingdon Library Quarterly*, xxvi (1963), 291–313.

Colin Clout begins with a Latin epigraph from Psalm 94.16 ('Who will rise up for me against the evildoers?', etc.), with the answer 'Nemo, Domine' (No one, O Lord). In 1–46, here omitted, the poet (in his 'persona' of the vagrant Goliardic 'clerk' speaking on behalf of the common people) despairs of effecting anything from his railing, teaching and preaching, and pretends to mock his own folly in writing satire.

51. *Conning.* Learning. The 'bag' is the vagrant's wallet.

69. *Hoder-moder.* Hugger-mugger.

293. *Clergy.* Learning. *Appose.* Procure.

298. *Simoniac.* One who practises simony (the buying and selling of benefices).

299. *Hermoniac.* Perhaps 'Armenian': see H. L. R. Edwards, *Times Literary Supplement*, 24 October 1936, p. 863.

316. *Rochets.* Vestments. Rennes, in Brittany, was then a centre for the manufacture of fine linen.

317. *White as morrow's milk.* Kinsman prefers the reading 'mare's milk', but cf. **19**, 22. *Morrow's.* This morning's.

319. *Begared.* Begarded, adorned.

324. *Jack of the Noke.* Common term for the 'man in the street'.

602. *Javel.* Rascal.

604. *Face.* Brag. *Crake.* Vaunt.

613. *Appal.* Dismay.

909. *Placebo.* Literally, 'I shall please' (cf. 911), but also the first word of the

163

first antiphon of the Roman Catholic Office of the Dead (parodied by Skelton at the beginning of *Philip Sparrow*). To 'sing placebo' was to be servile.

931. *Cross*. Coin (some of the coinage was stamped with a cross at this time).

932. *Predial lands*. Farm lands.

936ff. Refers to Wolsey's palace at Hampton Court.

940–1. Kinsman suggests that these lines should be transposed.

950. *Shoot a crow*. Shoot ineffectually, without killing.

951. *Tirly-tirlo*. Sexual euphemism.

956. *Bydene*. Collected together.

957. *Well beseen*. Of good appearance. This line is omitted in Henderson's text.

975. *Courage*. Desires.

982–1074. The whole of this passage is an attack on Wolsey, the 'president' of the King's Council.

983. *Remord*. Rebuke, criticize.

985. *Run*. Spread reports.

987. *Melling*. Meddling (cf. 1017, 1162).

999. *Rede*. Recommend.

1000–2. The meaning is: 'to be friendly with kings, to rule over all men, to misrule over yourself'. The reading 'pravare' may be corrupt.

1003. *Ure*. Hap, luck.

1025. *And not so hardy on his head*. And be not so rash as: an elliptical expression (cf. 1154).

1054. *Uncouths*. Strange matters.

1067. *Debetis scire*. 'You ought to know.'

1068. *Audire*. 'Hear.'

1069. *Convenire*. Meetings.

1070. *Praemunire*. This statute of 1393 (so called from the first word of the Latin writ) was a perpetual threat to the English clergy during the first part of the reign of Henry VIII. It could be invoked against anyone who submitted to ecclesiastical jurisdiction in matters which might be regarded as being within the authority of the king's courts. The penalty on conviction was forfeiture of goods and imprisonment. See A. F. Pollard, *Wolsey* (1929), pp. 245–50. By an irony which Skelton would have appreciated, it was under this statute that Wolsey himself was ultimately arraigned.

1075. *Mooting*. Chiding, arguing.

1076. *Gazing*. Henderson misreads 'gasping'. *Toting*. Peeping.

1098. *Escry*. Cry out against.

1106. *Disavailing*. Damaging.

1119ff. Alludes to Wolsey.

1134. *Deprave*. Defame.

1137. *Reciting*. Henderson misreads 'resting'.

1150. The meaning is that satire ('railing') has no effect on the wicked prelates, whose retaliation against those who have preached against them, and in particular the poet himself, is imagined in 1152ff. Skelton has, of course, Wolsey chiefly in mind.

1154. i.e. let them watch out for their heads (not be so rash). Cf. 1025.

1155. *Losel*. Good-for-nothing. Cf. 1163.

1156. *Weasand*. Throat.

1159. *Doctor Devyas.* A term of contempt, possibly a variant of 'Doctor Deuce-ace' in Nashe (*Works*, iii, 72); or from 'devious', erring.

1162. *Dawcock.* Simpleton. Cf. 'daw' in **9**, 913.

1170. *Lurden.* Clown.

1171. *Little Ease.* Prison.

1177. *Fee-simpleness.* Absolute possession (cf. **9**, 867): a punning reference to Wolsey's acquisitions of land (cf. note on praemunire, 1070).

1239–41. The poem was not printed until after Skelton's death; it circulated in MS.

1244. *Nolls.* Heads.

1245. *Noddy polls.* Silly heads.

1255. *Waves wood.* Raging waves.

1268. Here the poem ends, except for a colophon in Latin.

3, 4. See Introduction, pp. 15–16. Sir Thomas Wyatt, poet, courtier and diplomat (died 1542), wrote three satires, which were first printed (with many of his lyrics) in *Tottel's Miscellany* (1557). I follow K. Muir's edition (1949) in printing the earlier text found in the Egerton MS (but see note on **4**, 21).

3 (Muir no. 197). Addressed (see 70) to John Poynz, nephew of the statesman Sir Anthony Poynz. The philosophy of being content with one's lot is common in Horace, e.g. *Satires*, I i. The Aesopian fable is from Horace, *Satires*, II, vi (see Introduction, p. 1, and cf. Henryson's version, *The Taill of the Uponlandis Mous and the Burges Mous*).

26. *Cater.* Caterer.

48. *Purpose.* Conversation.

53. *Steaming eyes.* Cf. Chaucer, *Prologue*, A 202.

61. *Tho.* Then.

88. *Hay.* Hunting-net.

97. Cf. Persius, *Satires*, I, 7: 'nec te quaesiveris extra'.

100. *Mad.* You are mad. *Sore.* Suffering.

103. *All and some.* Everything.

105ff. Modelled on Persius *Satires*, III, 35ff.

4 (Muir no. 198). The most brilliant and ironical of Wyatt's satires, modelled from 28 onward on Horace, *Satires*, II, v, but without the mock-epic framework (see Introduction, p. 1). This satire is unusual in the Horatian canon (though cf. *Epistles*, I, vi) in that, to quote Fraenkel, 'it is no mirror of the poet's own life, nor does it aim at giving a picture of some part of human life in general. It is a caricature.' The structure is that of a dialogue in which the poet offers Sir Francis Brian (courtier, scholar and diplomat) mock-serious advice on how to get rich by abandoning honesty.

16. *Nappy.* Heady. Cf. **32**, 135.

18. *Groins.* Either 'grunts' or 'roots' (from ME 'groyn', snout).

21. I print Tottel's version of this line, since the Egerton reading ('Then of the harp the ass to hear the sound') obscures the intended parallel between two proverbial expressions. The poet has asked Brian why he does not stay at home in contented ignorance, to which he replies that he would then resemble the animals in the fables. The swine did not value the pearl (cf. Matthew, 7.6), the ass could not play the harp. The latter first occurs in the Latin verse fables of

Phaedrus (first century A.D.), who also has a chicken finding a pearl, and became familiar through Boethius (cf. Chaucer's *Boece*, I, prose 4,2). By the twelfth century it was a popular subject for illustration, both in carvings (e.g. in the church at Aulnay-de-Saintonge, France) and illumination (see C. R. Dodwell, *The Canterbury School of Illumination*, Cambridge, 1954, pp. 69–70).

45. *Cant*. Portion.
46. *Lese*. Lose.
47. *Kittson*. A rich bookseller.
57. *Withouten mo*. Without more ado.
61. *Rivelled*. Wrinkled.
63. *Ban*. Curse. For the tautology, cf. **7**, 37.
75. *Pandar*. Pandarus, in Chaucer's *Troilus and Criseide*.
78. *Price*. Value.
84. *Leve*. Allow.

5. See Introduction, pp. 2–5, 28. A translation of Horace, *Satires*, II, i, by Thomas Drant, from *A Medicinable Moral* (1566), the first English version of Horace's satires (he added the *Epistles* and *Art of Poetry* in 1567). Drant was educated at St John's College, Cambridge, became archdeacon of Lewes, and died in 1578. His attempts to draw up rules for English prosody based on classical quantitative principles are alluded to in the Spenser-Harvey correspondence. The poem is an 'apology' for writing satire in the form of a dialogue. Cf. **35**.

18. *Totty noll*. Muzzy head. The phrase also occurs in *The Faerie Queene*, VII, vii, 39.

33. Drant substitutes a character from English history for Horace's reference to Augustus's wars. His source was probably the *Mirror for Magistrates*.

37. *Lucile*. Lucilius. See Introduction, p. 3, and cf. **8**, 220ff.

47–8. Horace is here quoting from one of his own satires (I, viii) an instance of the kind of unheroic characters he writes about.

50. *Cons*. Show(s): this use of a singular verb where we should now use a plural is common in early Tudor verse.

63. *Stay*. Support.

71. Horace was born at Venusia (now Venosa) on the frontier between Apulia and Lucania.

81. *Style*. The Latin word 'stilus' means 'dagger' as well as 'pen' and 'way of writing'.

85. *Losels*. Cf. **2**, 1155.

101. *Canadie*. Canidia. Drant's transliteration of Latin proper names is somewhat capricious. Canidia was a witch who figures in one of Horace's epodes.

113. *Sheva*. Scaeva, of whom we know nothing except what Horace implies, that he poisoned his mother.

142. *Uneathes*. Uneasily.

143. *Lelie*. The consul Laelius.

144–6. Refers to Scipio Africanus.

163–4. This claim of Horace's ('tamen me cum magnis vixisse invita fatebitur usque invidia') is echoed by Ariosto in the last line of the passage quoted in the Introduction, p. 15.

179. *Of a zeal*. Zealously.

6, 7. From the collection commonly known as *Gude and Godlie Ballatis* (*Ane Compendious Buik of Godlie Psalmes*, etc.) consisting mainly of metrical hymns and psalms but also including a number of religious adaptations of secular songs and some satirical ballads. The earliest known edition was printed in Edinburgh in 1567 (reprinted, ed. A. F. Mitchell, for the Scottish Text Society, 1897). Probable date of composition, *c.* 1540. For reasons of conformity, the text has been anglicized.

7. A religious version of a popular hunting-song, with Christ substituted for Harry (Henry VIII), etc.

25. *Tantony bell.* St Anthony's bell: used of any small bell.
32. *Paltry.* Pedlar's ware, trash.
37. *Ban.* Curse. For the tautology, cf. **4**, 63.

8. See Introduction, pp. 16–17, 27. George Gascoigne (*c.* 1539–77), an Inns of Court man, M.P. and soldier, misspent his youth and tried to recover his fortunes through court patronage. He was one of the most important innovators among the early Elizabethan writers, in drama and prose as well as verse. *The Steel Glass* (published 1576), dedicated to Lord Gray of Wilton, is (like much of his verse) largely autobiographical. In the preface Gascoigne offers the work as an amendment for past follies and says that he has 'learnt in sacred scriptures to heap coals upon the head of mine enemies by honest dealing'. Complete text in the second volume of J. W. Cunliffe's edition of the *Poems* (Cambridge, 1910).

60. *Poesis.* Poetry.
84. *Make.* Mate.
104. *Bet.* Better.
107. *Silly.* Innocent.
128. *Wray.* Betray.
158. *Conceit.* Fancy.
161. At this point Gascoigne says in a prose marginal note 'the substance of the theme beginneth'.
166. *Surquedry.* Arrogance.
181. *Foils.* Backings to mirrors made of a thin layer of some metal or precious substance. The point of this passage is that a mirror backed with beryl or crystal would alter what is reflected in it, while one of steel (which is neutral) would not, so that Gascoigne's glass is a truthful one: a characteristic claim of the satirist.
193. *Rue.* Fall.
201. *Latter Lammas-day.* Never (since there is no such day).
208. *Lais.* Name often used by Elizabethan satirists for a courtesan: cf. **26**, 172.
220. Lucilius. See note on **5**, 37.

9. Edmund Spenser (died 1599) is most celebrated as the author of *The Faerie Queene. Prosopopoia: or Mother Hubberd's Tale* (the main title means personification) was probably written about 1579 and revised for publication in 1591. It is a long homiletic satire in neo-medieval style, falling into four sections, of which the third, against the court, is here given complete. Perhaps its most notable passages are the portrait of the ideal courtier (711–92) and the eloquent lines describing the miseries of those who seek advancement at court (892–908), inspired by the poet's own unrealized ambitions (see Introduction, p. 15). The animal symbolism is from Caxton's version of *Renard the Fox*. Complete text of **9** and **10**, with detailed commentary, in the *Variorum* Spenser, *The Minor Poems* (Baltimore, 2 vols., 1947). See also Introduction, pp. 1, 22, 27.

597. *Envy*. Pronounced in the medieval manner, with accent on the second syllable; cf. *enviest* in **10**, 678.

604. *Rede*. Inform.

620. *The wild beasts*. The Queen's soldier-courtiers.

622. *The Lion*. Elizabeth I.

626. *Buxom*. Obedient.

656. *Aguise*. Array.

668. *Countenance*. Demeanour. Cf. 846, 928.

671. *Mister wight*. Kind of man.

683. *Coverture*. Deceit.

699. *Leasings*. Lies. Cf. **1**, 96.

712. *Javel*. Rascal. Cf. **2**, 602.

714. *Fleer*. Sneer.

747. *Yewghen*. Made of yew.

781. *Amenance*. Behaviour.

785. *Interdeal*. Negotiations.

792. *Ekes*. Increases.

808. *Pandar*. See **4**, 75.

813. *Losel*. Good-for-nothing. Cf. **2**, 1155.

833. *Sectaries*. Disciples.

851. *Brocage*. Pimping.

852. *Borrow*. Security.

857. *Cleanly*. Artful. In 862 it is an adverb.

865. *Gage*. Pledge.

867. *Fee-simples*. Cf. **2**, 1177.

893. *Had y-wist*. Vain regret (literally 'had I known').

913. *Himself will a daw try*. Will prove himself a fool.

940. *Stound*. Trouble.

10. See Introduction, p. 18. The most autobiographical of Spenser's poems, written in Ireland in 1591 after an unsuccessful visit to London to seek a post at court; published 1595. The 'persona' of Colin Clout (also used in *The Faerie Queene*) is taken over from Skelton.

653. *Cynthia*. Elizabeth I.

696. *Leasings*. Cf. **1**, 96; **9**, 699.

701. *Filed*. Polished.

703. *Countenance*. Standing.

711. *Weed*. Dress.

744. *Ledden*. Speech.

747. *Wite*. Blame.

749. *General*. If applied generally.

757. *Most-what*. For the most part.

763. *Moldwarps*. Moles. *Nuzzling*. Burrowing.

767. *Ensue*. Follow. Cf. 'sue' in 786.

774. *Wonned*. Dwelt.

775ff. Spenser here attacks the debasement by courtiers of the ideal of love, as he does in *The Faerie Queene*.

783. *Lere*. Lore.

790. *Compliment*. Accomplishment. Cf. **16**, 44.

11. The descriptive title of this broadside ballad reads as follows: 'A most excellent godly new ballad: showing the manifold abuses of this wicked world, the intolerable pride of people, the wantonness of women, the dissimulation of flatterers, the filthiness of whoredom, the unthriftiness of gamesters, the cruelty of landlords, with a number of other inconveniences.' First registered 1586, re-issued 1624; reprinted by H. E. Rollins, *The Pack of Autolycus* (1927), pp. 3–6. To be sung to the tune 'Greensleeves'. (No. 7 in Rollins, *Analytical Index*, 1924.)

6. *Go*. Rollins reads 'Do'. The first letter is torn in the unique original copy.

26. *Cog*. Cheat.

31. *Guarded*. Trimmed. Cf. **2**, 319, **24**, 65.

75. *Boot*. Advantage.

12–15. See Introduction, *passim*. Thomas Lodge (1558–1625), an Inns of Court man who later abandoned literature for medicine, wrote prose as well as verse. His pastoral romance *Rosalynde* (1590) was used by Shakespeare for *As You Like It*, and his *Wit's Misery* (1596), a picaresque prose satire in the manner of Nashe, was used by Hall and Rowlands (see Notes on **20**, **29–31**). A selection of his poems is here printed from the original editions; page-references in the passages from *Wit's Misery* quoted in notes on **29–31** are to vol. iv of the 1883 edition of his *Works* (reprinted New York, 1963). Lodge is important in the history of verse-satire because he began in the homiletic manner and ended in the classical. For a survey of his life and works, see N. B. Paradise, *Thomas Lodge* (New Haven, 1931).

12. From *An Alarum Against Usurers* (1584), a miscellany in prose and verse 'containing tried experiences against worldly abuses'. The poem is a secularized and allegorized version of the traditional theme of Christ's complaint over Jerusalem. For the tone and stanza, which may have been influenced by Sackville's Induction to the 1563 edition of the *Mirror for Magistrates*, cf. **33**.

39. Britain was supposed to have got its name from its legendary founder, the Trojan Brutus, according to Geoffrey of Monmouth, whose medieval *History of the Kings of Britain* was still popular in Tudor times.

46. *Stour*. Place. Cf. 55.

51. *Novels*. New things.

60. *Suspect*. Suspicion. *Charely*. Carefully.

66. *Band*. Bond.

67. *Mel*. Honey.

87. *Wood*. Mad. Cf. **2**, 1255.

108. *Frame*. Direct, dispose. I have removed the full-stop with which this line ends in the original edition, but the sense of the stanza (which fails to preserve the rhyme-scheme) remains obscure. It may perhaps be paraphrased: 'truth must never compromise with the good. Good may be defined as what benefits princes, in pursuing which they also benefit their subjects. But the good I want is a common and absolute good, not mere material advantage.'

134. *When as*. When.

175. *Racked rents.* Rack-rents, extortionate rents: a common complaint of homiletic satire. For the singular verb with plural subject cf. **5**, 50; **13**, 52.

13. From *Scylla's Metamorphosis* (1589), a verse-miscellany the title-poem of which is an Ovidian 'epyllion'. For the 'satyre', see Introduction, p. 19, and for Philomel, p. 16.

    61. Refers to Alexander of Macedon, who conquered Darius (334 B.C.).

    62. *Vail.* Lower.

    73. *Tellus.* The Earth.

14. This anti-court poem, from the same collection as **13**, combines classical 'withdrawal' with Christian *contemptus mundi*. Like **12**, the poem invokes the mournful Muse Melpomene who speaks lines 7–18.

    7. *Forthy.* Therefore.

    29–30. Refers to Virgil, who appears in his first *Eclogue* as the 'shepherd' Tityrus.

    33. *Apaid.* Satisfied. Cf. 39.

    37. The Muses were the daughters of Memory and Apollo.

    67ff. For the pastoral imagery, cf. Introduction, pp. 19–20.

    81. *Steven.* Prayer.

15. The fifth satire (against discontent) from *A Fig For Momus* (1595), a collection of somewhat haphazardly arranged poems labelled either 'satires' or 'epistles': Lodge's last book of verse, in which he abandoned the stanzas and tone of homiletic satire and adopted the couplet together with the forms of classical satire, including the use of numbers instead of titles to designate each poem—thereby anticipating Hall by two years. The opening of this poem is from Juvenal, *Satires*, x; other models are Horace, *Satires*, I, i and *Epistles*, I, vi. Cf. also **22**.

    35. Some of Lodge's 'examples' are current types but Hepar may refer to Dr Lopez, the Portuguese-born physician to Queen Elizabeth I, who was executed for treason in 1594.

    61. Cf. Juvenal, *Satires*, x, 346.

    71. *Entapissed.* Carpeted.

    81. Pompey the Great was stabbed to death by his former centurion in 48 B.C.

16, 17. See Introduction, p. 14. John Donne (1572–1631) wrote a number of verse-letters and five satires, which circulated in MS, remaining unprinted until after his death (as did his more celebrated *Songs and Sonets*). The most recent edition is by W. Milgate (Oxford, 1967) who accepts the date 1593 for Satire I: if correct, this would make it the earliest specimen of the 'new satire' produced during the 1590s by the group of University and Inns of Court 'wits' who included Lodge, Hall, Marston and Guilpin. Donne (who was born a Catholic) later entered the Anglican church and became Dean of St Paul's.

16. The longest and most powerful of Donne's satires, written (see note on line 114) not earlier than 1597. Down to line 154 the model is Horace, *Satires*, I, ix (see Introduction, p. 3); 155–end are a general attack on the court (cf. **9**, 892–908) introducing a variety of characters (cf. **24**) and combining homiletic elements with 'Juvenalian' rhetoric.

3. Cf. 158.

10. 100 marks was the fine prescribed, under a statute of 1580, for attending Mass.

17. Here Donne begins his imitation of Horace.

18. For the myth of spontaneous generation in the mud of the Nile (Ovid, *Metamorphoses* I, 422–37), cf. *The Faerie Queene*, I, i, 21.

26. The London apprentices rioted against foreigners on several occasions.

35. For the *soi-disant* traveller, cf. **22, 29.**

41. *Drug-tongue*. Patter used by itinerant quacks.

44. *Complement*. Accomplishment. Cf. **10,** 790.

48. *Jovius, Surius*. Sixteenth-century Catholic historians whose accuracy was impugned by Protestants.

53. *Sillily*. Foolishly.

54. *Calepine*. Sixteenth-century Italian friar whose Latin dictionary later developed into a polyglot one.

55. *Beza*. Calvinist theologian.

56. A contemporary MS identifies these characters as John Reynolds of Corpus Christi College, Oxford, and Lancelot Andrewes, the celebrated divine.

59. *Panurge*. Comic character in Rabelais noted for his resourcefulness.

70. *Aretine*. Pietro Aretino (1492–1556), Italian poet notorious for his outspokenness and much admired by Elizabethan satirists, especially Nashe. Some of his erotic poems were illustrated by Giulio Romano, but the illustrations do not survive.

86. *Grogaram*. Grosgrain, a corded silk fabric.

87. *Pitch*. The height to which a trained hawk will fly: the satirist is the hawk but his prey eludes him.

97. Tudor chroniclers.

112. *Gallo-Belgicus*. An annual news-register.

114. The French lost Amiens to the Spaniards in March 1597 and recaptured it in September of the same year.

117. *Macaroon*. Fop or buffoon.

158. Refers to Dante (cf. the opening lines of the poem).

169. Refers to an artificial garden exhibited in London at this time.

171. *Flouts*. Mocks, parodies. *Presence*. The ceremonial attendance by the court on the monarch (cf. 179, 199).

176. Balloon: the game of 'pallone': see *Shakespeare's England*, ii, 462.

196. *Drugs*. Cosmetics.

197. *Macrine*. A courtier. Donne, Hall, Marston, all borrow 'type' names from classical verse-satire: this one occurs in Persius, *Satires*, II. For the reference to Heracleitus cf. Juvenal, *Satires*, x, 28–30, and Introduction, pp. 2 and 14.

199. *Moschite*. Mosque.

204. Dürer wrote a treatise on the proportions of the human body.

216. *Pursuivant*. Warrant-officer. An earlier reading is 'Topcliff', who was employed by the State to obtain confessions from Catholics under torture. Donne may well have decided, like Juvenal, that it was dangerous to name the living.

225–6. Refers to the medieval iconographic tradition according to which Christ's scourgers were depicted as personifications of evil.

233. *Ascapart*. A giant in the medieval romance of *Sir Bevis*: here referring to the Queen's bodyguard.

242–4. The book of Maccabees is classed as uncanonical.

17. For the verse-letter as a form of 'reflective satire' see Introduction, p. 4. The advice here given is similar to that in Horace, *Epistles*, I, xi ('caelum non animum mutant qui trans mare currunt') and Persius, *Satires*, IV ('tecum habita'). The court-city-country debate was a stock theme in the Renaissance. The addressee, Sir Henry Wotton, poet and diplomat, was secretary to the Earl of Essex and subsequently provost of Eton. Cf. also **39**.

8. *Remora*. The sucking-fish, so named from its supposed power to delay ships.

11. *Even*. Equinoctial (the equator). The meaning of this and the following lines is that, on a real voyage, though we may suffer from extremes of temperature we know that a temperate zone lies between; whereas on the voyage of life we can find no such refuge except (as the poet goes on to say) within ourselves.

26. The words in brackets mean that virtue, like all habits, is not inborn but acquired.

34. *Denizened*. Naturalized. *Barbarous*. Foreign.

59. *Galen*. Greek physician, second century B.C.

62. *Chemics*. Chemists.

70. For the pun on the poet's name, cf. the end of Donne's hymn 'To God the Father'.

18–23. See Introduction, pp. 21–3. Joseph Hall (1574–1656) was educated (as was Guilpin, see **27**) at Emmanuel College, Cambridge. Like Donne, he entered holy orders, subsequently becoming a bishop. For further details of his life, and of his place in English verse-satire, see the edition of his poems by A. Davenport (Liverpool, 1949). His satires, to which he gave the Latin title *Virgidemiae* ('Harvest of Scourges'), were printed in 1597 (books I–III) and 1598 (books IV–VI). (The prologue to book III is printed in the Introduction, p. 21.) In his prologue to book I (**18**) Hall claims to be the first English satirist. In fact, both Lodge and Donne anticipated him in the use of couplets and of classical models, but he was perhaps the first to make self-conscious use of the 'persona' of the 'satyre' as a 'scourge', in which he was followed by Marston. He borrows from Nashe and Lodge. His themes are mainly the stock targets of the day: braggarts, lawyers, upstarts, etc. He also attacks other writers.

19. An attack on the Petrarchan sonnet, one of a series of short satires in book I against other literary forms. Cf. Nashe, *Piers Penniless* (*Works*, i, 169).

24. *Refuse*. Worthless (adjective: cf. **22**, 15).

20. An attack on astrology. Again Hall claims to be the first in the field: but cf. Juvenal, *Satires*, VI, 532–91 (where, however, astrological beliefs are shown as typically feminine), Barclay, *Ship of Fools*, Nashe, *Have With You to Saffron Walden* (*Works*, iii, 72, 83–4), and Lodge, *Wit's Misery* (see note on **30**, 53ff.). Milton admired the opening of this poem, but disliked Hall's use of Cambridge place-names in 31–8, though he himself mentions the Bull in his poem on Hobson the Cambridge carrier. The inn-names are also signs of the Zodiac.

6. *Ephemerides*. Diary or calendar. Cf. Juvenal, *Satires*, VI, 674.

8. *Not . . . nor . . . nor*. Either . . . either . . . either. *Fatal horn*. i.e., when he is to be cuckolded.

19. *Pares his nails.* Cf. the passage by Lodge quoted in note on **30**, 53ff. *Libs.* Castrates.

23. Cf. Juvenal, *Satires*, VI, 571.

47. *Liver-sick.* The liver was thought by classical writers to be the seat of the affections: cf. Horace, *Odes*, IV, i, 12.

21. A burlesque on a drunkard, 'Gullio', who has not been identified.

3. *The ferryman of hell.* Charon (see Virgil, *Aeneid*, VI, 298ff.).

22. The motto-phrase means 'what then do people want?' (Horace, *Epistles*, II, i, 206). The theme of this satire is envy of other people's lot, a common one in Horace, e.g. *Satires*, I, i, and cf. note on **15**: Hall seems to have known Lodge's poem.

3. *Gades.* Cadiz. The phrase 'from Gades to the east', for the whole known world, occurs in Juvenal, *Satires*, X, 1; and cf. **15**, 1.

6. *Caenis.* A woman who changed her sex to avoid unwelcome lovers.

9–10. *Partlet.* A garment which covered the neck and breasts. *Busk.* A kind of stay. *Farthingale.* A device for making skirts stand out from the body. Women's fashions were a favourite target for satire in the 1590s (cf. **24** and **26**).

11. This line means that young men wear women's high-heeled shoes (made of cork) so can only take short steps like fettered convicts.

15. *Refuse.* Worthless. Cf. **19**, 24.

17. *Rock.* Distaff.

18. *Stock.* Either 'sword' (Italian *stocco*), in which case 'foreign' means non-native; or 'hose', in which case 'foreign' means designed for the other sex.

21. *Pannel.* Saddle.

24. The stockpiling of corn against a rise in the market was a common malpractice.

27. *Foist.* Cheat. *Strike.* Dry-goods measure.

36ff. Cf. Horace, *Satires*, I, i, 1–10, and Nashe, *Piers Penniless* (*Works*, i, 170–2).

41. *Cockers.* High leather boots or leggings such as are still worn by farmers.

43. *Fettleth.* Gets ready to go.

48–9. Cf. Virgil, *Georgics*, ii, 458–9.

50. Refers to the poet Elderton, for whom see note on **27**, 112.

53. *Handsel* (or hansel). First attempt.

54. *Wheel . . . pail.* A reference to women spinning and milking.

55. *Thraves.* Bundles.

58–81. For the teller of travellers' tales, cf. Nashe, *Piers Penniless* (i, 169): 'he will tell a whole legend of lies of his travels unto Constantinople'; cf. also note on **29**, 73ff., and *The Defence of Cony-Catching* (1592): 'this gentleman, forsooth, haunteth tabling-houses, taverns and such places, where young novices resort . . . and openly shadoweth his disguise with the name of traveller . . . then shall you hear him vaunt of his travels and tell what wonders he hath seen in strange countries . . . never having stepped a foot out of England.' (Cf. note on **28**.) Geographers and explorers had previously been satirized in *The Ship of Fools*.

60. *Spanish Decades.* A book of Spanish travels (including Columbus's) first published in 1516 and translated into English in 1555 and 1577.

61. *Mandeville.* Famous medieval travel-book.

73. *City of the Trinity.* Alexandria.

76. *Grasshopper*. The Royal Exchange. The device of its founder, Sir Thomas Gresham.

79. *Sithes*. Times.

23. Hall's most outspoken satire, against Roman Catholicism. The Greek motto is from a Sibylline oracle which prophesied (in a typical piece of word-play) that Rome would become 'rume' (a country lane).

9. *Aquine*. Juvenal, to whose *Satires*, x, 33ff., Hall here alludes.

19. *Pantheon*. Temple in Rome which became a Christian church.

27. *Cowls*. Monks. Hall alludes to the belief that brothels contributed to the papal revenue.

32. *Theatine*. Member of a congregation of 'regular clerks' founded in 1524.

42. *Valentine*. Refers to Nashe's obscene verse-satire *The Choice of Valentines* (printed in *Works*, iii, 397).

44. *Jacobite*. Member of an early heretical sect.

48. *Channel*. Gutter. Cf. **1**, 57.

53. *Acolythite*. Acolyte.

57. *Likerous*. Lustful (as in Chaucer).

67. The 'female father' was Pope Joan, who according to legend was a woman and who gave birth (hence 'yeaning' in 68) during a papal procession, so that all future popes were tested for sex in a 'trial chair'—a precaution rendered superfluous by the licentious popes of the Renaissance.

73. *Codro*. Refers to Juvenal, *Satires*, i, 2, in which the satirist (who is still the 'he' referred to by Hall) cries out against Codrus's tedious poems.

24–6. See Introduction, pp. 2, 8, 24. John Marston, poet and dramatist (1576–1634), a member of the Inner Temple, published two books of verse-satire in 1598, from the second of which, *The Scourge of Villainy*, the poems here printed are taken. This volume contains ten satires (eleven in the second edition, 1599) divided into three 'books' but numbered straight through (on the model of Juvenal). Marston's violent rhetoric and eccentric vocabulary were parodied both on the stage and by other verse-satirists (see **32**). But his outlook, temperament and verbal effects influenced the whole of Jacobean 'malcontent' drama; see the edition of his *Poems* by A. Davenport (Liverpool, 1961), introduction, pp. 11–30.

24. Supposedly a dialogue between the cynic Diogenes and 'Linceus' (the Argonaut proverbial for his keen sight), alluded to as a 'persona' of the satirist by Nashe, *Works*, iii, 218–19: 'say that a more piercing Linceus sight should dive into the entrails of this insinuating parasite's knavery'. The finest of Marston's satires, and the one in which we draw closest to the world of *Hamlet* and *King Lear*. The basic pattern of the encounter with a single satirized type (cf. **16**) is here developed into a parade or gallery of knaves.

1. A parody of *Richard III*, v. iv. 7.

6. *Samian saws*. The teachings of Pythagoras of Samos, who believed in the transmigration of human souls into animals (cf. the reference to Circe in 4–5).

62–5. Borrowed from Nashe (*Works*, i, 162).

63. Cato of Utica was a proverbial symbol of republican virtue.

65. *Budge*. Lamb's wool. *Guards*. Trimmings (cf. **11**, 31).

66. *The Stagirite*. Aristotle, whose classification of the soul is here referred to.

8off. Cf. Nashe (*Works*, iii, 213–17).

81. Imaginary names (like Richard Roe and John Doe) used by lawyers of the parties in a law-suit but here used of the lawyers themselves. Cf. **2**, 324.

85. *Blacksaunt*. Burlesque of a sacred song. *Geat*. Goth.

87. *Stoppels*. Estoppels. For these legal terms, see *O.E.D.*

94. *Astraea*. Personification of justice (cf. Juvenal, *Satires*, VI, 19).

95. *Megaeras*. Furies.

98. *Irus*. The town beggar in *Odyssey*, XVIII, who became proverbial for poverty.

101. For the Mavortian or Martialist (man born under Mars) cf. William Rankins, *Seven Satyres* (1598), II, 14: 'and swears he fought with monsieur hand in hand'.

108. *The Great Man's Head*. An inn (perhaps the Saracen's Head).

109. *Brill*. Dutch town then garrisoned by the British.

112. *'ringo*. The root of the eryngo (sea-holly) used as an aphrodisiac.

128. *Naples pestilence*. Syphilis.

134. *Occupant*. Harlot.

143. *Tissue-slop*. Pair of baggy breeches made of rich cloth. *Panes*. Strips of cloth used for sleeves.

153. *Apaid*. Cf. **14**, 33.

167. *Surphuled*. Made up, painted.

168–9. *Under one hood two faces*. Proverbial expression for duplicity.

174. *Busk*. Stays. Cf. **22**, 9–10.

177. *Rebato*. The wire frame supporting a high collar.

179. *Preciseness*. Puritan primness.

185. The Esquiline Gate in Rome was used as a rubbish-dump. Cf. **26**, 200.

188ff. Cf. the end of **26**. The distinction between man and the lower animals was a commonplace of medieval and renaissance philosophy. Juvenal has a similar passage at the end of *Satires*, XV.

201. i.e.: 'we have senses like the animals, we grow like plants, we exist like stones, but we lack the distinctive human quality of understanding'.

25. The reference in line 20 is to the cleansing of the stables of Augeas by Hercules, the fifth of his twelve labours.

26. Curio is a type-name for the decadent courtier.

9ff. Cf. the lines of Guilpin quoted in Introduction, p. 24.

23–6. A parody of Virgil, *Aeneid*, II, 6–8.

26–8. Jove (pretending to be her husband Amphitryon) slept with Alcmena, who bore a son, Hercules.

34. Cf. Jonson's line on Hercules, **37**, 31.

35. *Crazed*. Broken.

37. *Surphuled*. Cf. **24**, 167.

44–8. These lines may be an echo of some lines in S. Taylor, *A Whip for Worldlings*, quoted in J. Peter, *Complaint and Satire*, pp. 131–2. A common source is Horace, *Odes*, II, x, 9–10.

56. Refers to Adonis. *Cyprian*. Refers to Venus.

57. *Streak*. Stretch. *Incensing*. Inflaming, amorous.

62. *Bacchis*. A courtesan.

74. *Lais.* A courtesan. Cf. 172 and **8**, 208.

94. *Busk-point.* The ribbon on the 'points' of a woman's stays. Cf. 118 and **24**, 174.

108. *Lin.* Leave off.

119. *Lusk.* Lurk. Also in 199.

131. *Farthingale.* See note on **22**, 9–10. This fashion, like the ruff, came in during the 1580s and was often satirized.

153ff. Refers to Jupiter's love for Europa; his first wife Metis is here referred to in the accusative because Marston is quoting from a favourite Latin source, the *Mythologia* of Natalis Comes (see Davenport, pp. 29–30).

173ff. Cf. note on **24**, 188ff. The philosophy of this passage is from Epictetus and Virgil (*Aeneid*, VI, 724ff.).

181. *Pegase.* Pegasus (winged horse in classical mythology). *Fantasy.* Soaring speculation.

200. *Port Esquiline.* Cf. **24**, 185.

211. *Synderesis.* Conscience. Cf. Jonson, *Every Man Out of His Humour*, III. i, where Clove says, parodying Marston: 'Now sir, whereas the ingenuity of the time and the soul's synderesis are but the embryons in nature, added to the paunch of the Esquiline and the intervallum of the zodiac . . .'

27. See Introduction, pp. 5, 24. Everard Guilpin matriculated at Emmanuel College, Cambridge, in 1588, the year before Hall. He was an Inns of Court man like Donne and Marston, both of whom influenced him. For what is known of his life, see Davenport's edition of Marston, pp. 2–3; *Review of English Studies*, xv (1939), 66–72; *Review of English Studies*, xiv (1963), 164–6; *Review of English Studies*, xvi (1965), 396–9. *Skialetheia* ('Truth's shadow'), his only book, was printed in 1598 (reprinted by G. B. Harrison as a Shakespeare Association facsimile, 1931): it is a collection of epigrams followed by six satires, of which no. 5 is here printed: its opening lines suggest that Guilpin may have read Donne's first satire in MS (compare the passage from this poem printed in Introduction, p. 14): cf. also **16**, **24**. Guilpin was attacked, with Marston, by Weever in *The Whipping of the Satyre* (1601) and replied in *The Whipping of the Satyre: his penance.* See also notes on **32**, **33**, and A. Davenport's edition of the 'Whipper' pamphlets (Liverpool, 1951).

15. Refers to Aristotle. Cf. **24**, 66.

28–30. The Rose theatre was in Southwark, the Curtain in Shoreditch. The Spaniard is Seneca.

42. *Blacksaunts.* See note on **24**, 85.

54. *Cony-catching.* See note on **28**.

56. *Kemp's jig.* William Kemp was a famous comic actor; a jig was a kind of comic sketch, sung and danced to ballad measure. *The Burgonian.* John Barrose, a Burgundian fencer, hanged in London in 1598. References to both these topical ballads also occur in Marston, *Scourge of Villainy*, XI.

57. *Nipped a bong.* 'Stolen a purse' (thieves' slang).

63–4. An echo of Juvenal, *Satires*, II, 8–9 (Latin text quoted in Introduction, p. 7).

68. *Walk in Paul's.* See note on **28**.

95. *Intelligencer.* Spy, informer.

96. *King Arthur's fencer.* An allusion to the jousts and tournaments in fencing

and archery held at Smithfield by a club calling itself 'Prince Arthur's knights'. See *Shakespeare's England*, ii, 385, 391.

98. *Sergeant*. High officer of the Court or Parliament. *Muff*. German or Swiss.

104. *Gue*. An actor or clown. Guilpin addresses one of his epigrams to him, referring again to his 'apishness'.

112. *Elderton*. Prolific writer of ballads, notorious for his drunkenness. Cf. **22**, 50.

114. *Don Pacolet*. A dwarf, in the medieval romance of *Valentine and Orson*, who made a magic wooden horse.

117. *Pace*. Refers to John Pace (died *c*. 1590), a professional jester who was forbidden the court by Elizabeth I because of his bitter jokes.

123. *Puisne*. Law student. The French original of the English word 'puny'. Cf. 163.

145. *Synomic*. Synonymic, full of synonyms. Cicero (Tully) was proverbial for his eloquence.

146. An allusion to a popular Tudor anthology, *A Gorgeous Gallery of Gallant Inventions*.

147. *Castilio*. Castiglione, author of *The Courtier*, a standard Renaissance work on the qualities and activities of the ideal courtier.

165. *Ordinary*. Eating-house.

28. No. 4 of *Micro-cynicon: six snarling satyres* (1599). Authorship uncertain: perhaps either Thomas Middleton or Thomas Moffat. Despite the self-consciously aggressive sub-title, these poems have little in common with the work of Marston or Hall; the poem here printed is a versified anecdote of the kind familiar in the prose of Nashe, Lodge and Greene: the last-named exposed the techniques of the 'cony-catchers' or confidence-tricksters in a series of pamphlets published 1591–2: reprinted by A. V. Judges, *The Elizabethan Underworld*, pp. 119–264. A 'cony' (also spelt coney or cunny) was a dupe or 'mug'. 'Paul's' (also spelt Powles), the scene of the 'pick-up', refers to the middle aisle of the old cathedral, a favourite haunt at this time of disreputable characters: cf. **27**, 68ff. Jonson sets some of the action of *Every Man Out of His Humour* in the 'middle aisle'.

3. *Jets*. Struts. A favourite word of satirists at this period: cf. **32**, 99; **34**, 409.

35. *Cates*. Choice food. Cf. **36**, 8.

29–31. From *The Letting of Humour's Blood in the Head-Vein* (1600), a collection consisting of some epigrams and six satires, by Samuel Rowlands (*c*. 1570–1628). His complete works (he subsequently published many other volumes) were edited for the Hunterian Society (3 vols., Glasgow, 1880), with notes and glossary by S. J. R. Herrtage. These satires are picaresque character-sketches in the manner of Hall and Guilpin; several passages are closely modelled on Lodge's *Wit's Misery* (see notes on Lodge and on **20**, **22**): some of these parallels were first noted by A. Davenport, *Notes and Queries*, 184 (1943), 13–16.

29. For the opening phrase 'Who have we here?', a common formula in contemporary prose writers, cf. **27**, 139.

10. The Centaurs were children of Ixion and Juno (the latter in the form of a cloud).

24. *Ordinary*. Cf. **27**, 165.

37. *Conceit*. Imagination.

42. *Baitless*. Without refreshment.

73ff. For the travellers' tales cf. **22**, 58ff. Some of the details are common to various travel-writers from Pliny to Mandeville, but the immediate source is Lodge (*Works*, iv, 35): 'He will tell you of monsters that have faces in their breasts, and men that cover their bodies with their feet instead of a penthouse. . . . He hath . . . the stone the devil offered Christ to make bread on . . . a piece of Caesar's chair wherein he was slain in the senate-house. He . . . was at the hanging of that fellow that could drink up a whole barrel of beer without a-breathing.'

30.

34ff. Cf. Lodge (*Works*, iv, 40–1): 'A devil called Dicing . . . he like a gallant haunts the cockpits. . . . This fellow is excellent at a bum-card. . . . He can burn the knave of clubs and find him in his bosom . . . he hath cards for the nonce for Primavista, others for Sant, others for Primero. . . . Whensoever he deals, you shall be sure of no good dealing. As for dice, he hath all kinds of fortes, fulhams, langrets, barred quarter-treys, high men, low men, some stopped with quicksilver . . . and ere he will want money for "Come on, five!" he will have it by five and a reach, or hang for it.' But the common source for both writers is the pamphlet *A Manifest Detection of . . . Dice-play*, etc., probably written by Gilbert Walker (*c.* 1580) and reprinted by A. V. Judges, *The Elizabethan Underworld*, pp. 26–50. For the various kinds of loaded dice, see *O.E.D.* and *Shakespeare's England*, ii, 469–71. *Saunt* (sant, sent) was a kind of piquet. *Mumchance* was a kind of hazard, but *Michel Mumchance* is a reference to another pamphlet, *Mihil Mumchance, his discovery of the art of cheating in false dice-play* (1597).

53ff. For the superstitious man, see note on **20**. Lodge (iv, 11–12) is a common source, but Rowlands borrows more details than Hall: 'Curiosity . . . setteth his mind wholly on astrology, necromancy and magic. . . . If you long to know this slave, you shall never take him without a book of characters in his bosom. . . . He will not eat his dinner before he hath looked in his almanack, nor pare his nails while Monday. . . . He will show you the devil in a crystal . . . and swearing to enrich the world in a month he is not able to buy himself a new cloak in a whole year.'

31.

14ff. Alludes to Greene's pamphlet *A Quip for an Upstart Courtier, or a quaint dispute between velvet and cloth breeches* (1592).

27–42. Some of these rustic games are described in *Shakespeare's England*, ii, 451–83, which quotes this passage; see also Strutt's *Sports and Pastimes of the People of England* (rev. J. C. Cox, 1903). *Hot cockles* was a blindfold guessing game; *Dun is in the mire* was played with a log of wood (representing Dun the cart-horse); *Irish* resembled backgammon; *Noddy* was like cribbage.

32. For John Weever, poet and antiquary (1576–1632), see *D.N.B.* His works include a collection of epigrams (1599) on Shakespeare and other literary contemporaries; *Faunus and Melliflora* (1600), a miscellany of erotic and satirical pieces, original and translated, from which this 'prophecy', really a satirical parody of Marston (see Introduction, p. 25), is taken; and *The Whipping of the Satyre* (1601), for which see note on **27**. The last two volumes have been edited by A. Davenport (Liverpool, 1948, 1951).

1–9. Refers to Marston and his circle, the 'followers of Lucilius' (see Introduction. p. 5). In the 'proemium' to *The Scourge of Villainy*, I, Marston claimed to 'bear the scourge of just Rhamnusia' (Nemesis). The sharp-eyed snakes of Epidaurus—another image for the all-penetrating satirist—are mentioned by Horace in *Satires*, I, iii, 26.

15. *Great Plato's year*. The *annus magnus platonicus*: the year (variously computed by ancient writers) in which all the heavenly bodies return to their original positions, thus completing a cycle. Weever links this idea with the Christian institution of the Jubilee year (see 68 and the article 'Jubilee' in the *Catholic Encyclopedia*).

33. *Dreriments*. Griefs.

36. *Enaunter*. In case.

39. *Bourd*. Mockery.

50. *Aretine*. Cf. **16**, 70.

52. Cf. Marston, *Scourge of Villainy*, III, 121, where Leuca appears as Lucea.

57. *Picthatch*. Haunt of prostitutes in Clerkenwell, also mentioned by Marston and Jonson.

59–60. Refers to Marston's 'Cynic' satire (**24**).

75. *Saturnus*. The reign of Saturn was the golden age. Cf. **39**, 50.

91. *Puisnes*. Cf. note on **27**, 122. *Fry*. Junior.

99. *Jet*. Cf. **28**, 3.

133. *Ysking*. (? ishing). Uttering (Davenport).

134. *Scale*. Davenport says: '? Danish from "skoal"'; a more probable explanation of the line is that the cup in the drunkard's hands is 'slupped' (slopped) unsteadily up and down like a scale-pan.

150. Refers to Cicero's famous cry 'O tempora o mores' in his first oration against Catiline.

33. Nicholas Breton (*c.* 1551–1623), stepson of George Gascoigne, had a long and prolific literary career; his works range from lyrics to romantic fiction. Beginning in 1600 he published a series of satires using the 'persona' of Pasquil, following Nashe (see J. Peter, *Complaint and Satire in Early English Literature*, p. 119). These poems are homiletic in the earlier manner of Lodge (cf. **12**, **13**) and are generally much longer than the piece here printed, from *Melancholic Humours*, 1600 (reprinted, with an essay on Elizabethan melancholy, by G. B. Harrison, 1929). J. Peter has suggested (op. cit., 151–2) that Breton wished to dissociate himself from the recently banned aggressive satires, written in couplets, of Marston and Guilpin (for which he evidently had no aptitude anyway) by reverting to the old-fashioned tone and stanza of 'complaint'. Breton also contributed a characteristically protracted refutation of Weever's 'Whipper' satire (see notes on **27**, **32**). See also *Review of English Studies*, xvii (1941), 80–6. Breton's *Works* were edited by A. B. Grosart in 1879 but more poems have since come to light.

12. *Cheer*. Aspect.

17. *Wears*. Wears itself out.

24. *Where that*. Where.

32. For this proverbial expression, cf. **24**, 168–9.

44. *That*. That which.

46–7. i.e.: 'wit and reason will not be able to put into your mind any thought that will not somehow torment you'.

66. *Bands.* Bonds. Cf. **12**, 66. Refers to pacts with the devil.

72. *All but.* Nothing but.

79. *Summer flies.* Fair-weather friends. Cf. Herbert's sonnet 'The Answer', 4–5.

34. Of Richard Middleton nothing seems to be known. *Epigrams and Satyres* (1608) is his only recorded work: despite its title it contains only one satire, 'Time's Metamorphosis', of which the last two sections are here printed from the copy of the first edition in the Edinburgh University Library. J. Peter has suggested (*Complaint and Satire in Early English Literature*, p. 165) that each section of this long work is virtually a separate poem (it is so printed in the original edition). The poem is a covert satire (cf. **32**) and ends with the poet repudiating a 'Juvenalian' persona in favour of a 'Horatian' one. The Latin motto ('times change and we with them') was popular with the Elizabethans and was often attributed to Ovid (who has 'omnia mutantur' in *Metamorphoses*, xv, 165, and cf. also *Fasti*, vi, 771), but is not classical: it has not so far been found to occur earlier than 1566 (see H. Walther, *Proverbia sententiaeque latinitatis medii aevi*, vol. v, Gottingen 1967, no. 31206).

384. *Object.* Abject.

396. *Ding.* Precipitate violently.

409. *Jet.* Strut. Cf. **28**, 3.

410. *Vail bonnet.* Take their hat off.

423–4. The meaning is that paradoxes and contradictions previously apparent in Middleton's writing (antiphrasis is a rhetorical term) will now be seen to be true, since time has confirmed them.

451–2. *Revolutions . . . retrogradians.* Mutations and deteriorations (astrological).

35–39. Ben Jonson (1572–1637), poet and dramatist, was one of the great English classicists of his age. With the exception of **35**, all the poems here printed were first published in the two collections entitled *Epigrams* and *The Forest* (1616): the latter title is a translation of the Latin *Silvae*, a collection of miscellaneous poems. For the Jonsonian epigram, see Introduction, p. 10. Texts in the Muses Library edition, ed. G. B. Johnston (1954) and C. H. Herford and P. Simpson's *Ben Jonson*, vols. viii (1947) (text) and xi (1952) (commentary).

35. Translation of Horace, *Satires*, ii, i (cf. **5**). See Herford and Simpson, iv (1932) (text) and ix (1950) (commentary). Added by Jonson to the end of Act III of the 1616 edition of his play *The Poetaster*. He had been attacked for his satire (cf. the opening lines of *Forest*, xiii, quoted in Introduction, p. 23), and evidently wished to defend himself by reminding his critics of how Horace had dealt with similar charges. In the epilogue to *The Poetaster* he says he chose

Augustus Caesar's times
To show that Virgil, Horace and the rest
Of those great master-spirits did not want
Detractors.

23. *Burst.* Broken.

57. *Not.* Know not. Cf. note on **5**, 71 ff., for this autobiographical passage.

65. *Style*. See note on **5**, 81.
73. *Disease*. Annoyance.
103. *The man*. Lucilius.
107–8. Cf. **5**, 144.
109. *Storm*. Complain.
119–20. Cf. **5**, 163.

36. *Epigrams*, CI. The 'modest repast' was a favourite theme of classical reflective satire. The models are Horace, *Epistles*, I, v, Juvenal, *Satires*, XI, 56–end, and Martial, *Epigrams*, v, lxxviii, x, xlviii, XI, lii.
  8. *Cates*. Cf. **28**, 35.
  17. *And lie, so you will come*. Martial's 'mentiar, ut venias'. (XI, lii, 13).
  20. *Knat, rail*. Kinds of bird. *Ruff*. Bream.
  36. Robert Poley was 'by' at the supper-party which ended with Marlowe's death. Parrot was presumably another informer.

37. *Epigrams*, CXIII. A burlesque of Aeneas's visit to the underworld (see Introduction, p. 1). Jonson's mock-epic tone and use of joke-rhymes (borrowed from Italian satire) offer occasional curious anticipations of Byron. The Fleet Ditch, scene of the voyage, ran from Holborn to the Thames.
  3–4. Refers to Aeneas.
  13–14. References to Aristophanes's burlesque of an underworld journey in *The Frogs*, and to the dog Cerberus who guarded the entrance to the underworld (Virgil, *Aeneid*, VI, 417–25).
  The Voyage Itself
  15ff. Refer to the various 'stunt' journeys popular at this time, including that of Kemp the actor who danced from London to Norwich in 1599 and wrote an account of his journey in the *Nine Days Wonder* (1600).
  30. *Alcides*. Hercules, here invoked because he descended into the underworld.
  31. Possibly echoing a line of Marston (cf. **26**, 34).
  41. *In the first jaws*. Virgil's 'primis in faucibus' (*Aeneid*, VI, 273).
  54. *The ox in Livy*. Said (Bk. xxxv, Ch. xxi) to have uttered a warning to Rome.
  64. The trull is Scylla; but the one who cut off her father's hair was a different Scylla from the one who was turned into the rock opposite Charybdis (see Ovid, *Metamorphoses*, VIII and XIV).
  92. *Polypheme*. The Cyclops in Homer's *Odyssey*, IX.
  100. *Foist*. State barge.
  108. *Nicholas Hill*. An Oxford philosopher.
  126. *Houghs*. Hocks.
  135. *Tiberts*. Cats (so named in *Renard the Fox*).
  154. Refers to the London church of St Sepulchre.
  176. Refers to Sir John Harington, author of *The Metamorphosis of Ajax* (1596). Ajax is a pun referring both to the 'jakes' and to Homer's hero.

38. *Forest*, II. This poem describes the Sidney estate at Penshurst, Kent. The chief model is Martial, *Epigrams*, III, lviii. See also Introduction, p. 14; G. R. Hibbard, 'The English Country-house poem in the 17th century', in *Essential Articles for the Study of Alexander Pope*, ed. Maynard Mack (reprinted 1968), pp. 439–75; and K. W. Gransden, 'The Pastoral Alternative', in *Arethusa* (1970), 3.1, 3.2.

2. *Touch*. Precious metals (literally, the *quality* of gold or silver tested by the touchstone and then hallmarked). Cf. *Forest*, XII, 44.

14. Refers to the birth of Sir Philip Sidney. 'Sidney's oak' still exists.

19. Barbara Gamage married Lord Sidney in 1584.

26. These copses still exist.

29–44. In these lines Jonson looks forward to the nature-poetry, at once witty and deeply felt, of Marvell.

73. *Livery*. Provisions.

77. *The Prince*. James I's eldest son, Henry, died in 1612.

78. *As*. As if.

90–1. Cf. Virgil, *Georgics*, II, 523–4.

39. *Forest*, III. For the verse-letter cf. **17** and see Introduction, p. 17. Sir Robert Wroth, who married into the Sidney family, had estates in Middlesex (Enfield) and Essex (Loughton): hence 'near the city and the court', 3. The models for this poem are Martial, *Epigrams*, I, xlix, Virgil, *Georgics*, II, 458ff. (for the picture of the golden age, also alluded to in the previous poem), Horace, *Odes*, II, xviii and *Epodes*, II, and (for lines 95–end) Juvenal, *Satires*, X, 346–end (see Introduction, pp. 7–8).

13. *Securer rest*. Virgil's 'secura quies' (*Georgics*, II, 467).

14. *Unbought*. Horace's 'inemptas' (*Epodes*, II, 48).

19. *Courteous*. Cf. note to **38**, 29–44, and Marvell, *Upon Appleton House*, 616.

37. *The whilst*. During which time.

43–4. Virgil, *Georgics*, II, 516–20.

50. *Saturn's reign*. The golden age: see also 63–4 and Virgil, *Georgics*, II, 536–8 and cf. **32**, 75.

61. *Leese*. Lose.

96. Cf. Juvenal, *Satires*, X, 350: 'carior est illis homo quam sibi'.

102. Cf. Juvenal, *Satires*, X, 356: 'mens sana in corpore sano'.

106. *Lent*. Latin usage (*creditum*): cf. Horace, *Odes*, I, xxiv, 11.

182